The Essence of Majorca:A Travel

Preparation Guide

Alexander Becker

INTRODUCTION

Welcome to the enchanting island of Majorca, a Mediterranean paradise that beckons travelers with its sun-kissed shores, rich history, and vibrant culture. Nestled in the Balearic archipelago, Majorca is renowned for its stunning landscapes, from pristine beaches to rugged mountains, offering a diverse range of experiences for every type of adventurer. Whether you're seeking relaxation, adventure, or a taste of Spanish charm, this Majorca travel guide will be your compass to navigate this captivating island and uncover its hidden gems. Join us on a journey through Majorca's captivating history, its picturesque towns, delectable cuisine, and the countless activities that await you on this Mediterranean jewel.

CHAPTER ONE

Introduction to Majorca

•*About Majorca*

Majorca, also known as Mallorca, is a jewel in the Mediterranean Sea and one of Spain's most popular tourist destinations. This beautiful island offers a diverse range of experiences, from its stunning beaches and vibrant nightlife to its rich history and picturesque landscapes. In this comprehensive travel guide, we'll delve into the various aspects of Majorca, helping you plan an unforgettable visit.

Geography and Climate

Majorca is the largest of the Balearic Islands, situated in the western Mediterranean. Its geography is diverse, featuring rugged mountain ranges, fertile plains, and a picturesque coastline. The Tramuntana Mountains, a UNESCO World Heritage Site, dominate the northwest, offering excellent hiking opportunities and breathtaking views.

The island enjoys a Mediterranean climate with hot, dry summers and mild, wet winters. Summer, from June to September, is the peak tourist season, with temperatures often exceeding 30°C (86°F). Spring and autumn are ideal for those seeking milder weather and fewer crowds.

Getting There and Around

Majorca is well-connected by air, with Palma de Mallorca Airport serving as the primary gateway. Numerous airlines offer direct flights from major European cities. Once on the island, you can explore it by renting a car, using public buses, or relying on taxis. There's also a well-developed network of cycling paths for the more adventurous travelers.

Accommodation

Majorca boasts a wide range of accommodation options to suit all budgets and preferences. Palma, the capital city, offers luxury hotels and boutique stays, while coastal towns like Magaluf and Palma Nova provide affordable resorts and apartments. For a more authentic experience, consider renting a rural villa or farmhouse in the interior.

Top Attractions

Palma de Mallorca: The capital city is a vibrant hub of culture, history, and shopping. Explore the stunning Cathedral of Santa Maria, visit the Royal Palace of La Almudaina, and stroll through the charming old town.

Beaches: Majorca is renowned for its pristine beaches. Cala Millor, Cala d'Or, and Playa de Muro are just a few of the many options for sunbathing and water sports.

Serra de Tramuntana: Nature lovers and hikers will be enthralled by this mountain range. Don't miss the picturesque village of Valldemossa and the dramatic Torrent de Pareis canyon.

Caves of Drach: Explore underground caves with stunning stalactites and an underground lake where classical music concerts are held.

Formentor Peninsula: Located in the far north, this area offers dramatic cliffs, beautiful beaches, and the iconic Formentor lighthouse.

Activities

Majorca offers a plethora of activities for all interests:

Water Sports: From scuba diving and snorkeling to windsurfing and sailing, the island's clear waters are a playground for aquatic enthusiasts.

Golf: Majorca boasts numerous golf courses with beautiful Mediterranean views.

Cycling: The island is a popular destination for cyclists, with challenging mountain routes and scenic coastal paths.

Wine Tasting: Discover Majorca's burgeoning wine scene by visiting local vineyards and tasting traditional wines.

Nightlife: Majorca has a lively nightlife scene, with clubs and bars open late into the night, particularly in Palma and Magaluf.

Cuisine

Majorcan cuisine is a delightful blend of Mediterranean and Spanish flavors. Try the famous "ensaimada," a sweet pastry, and savor seafood dishes like "paella" and "arroz brut." Don't forget to sample local wines and "hierbas," a traditional herbal liqueur.

Culture and Festivals

Majorca's culture is deeply influenced by its history and Mediterranean location. The island celebrates various festivals throughout the year, including Sant Antoni (January), Sant Joan (June), and La Beata (September). These events feature parades, music, and traditional dancing.

Shopping

Palma offers excellent shopping opportunities, from high-end boutiques to local markets. Don't forget to pick up handmade ceramics, pearls, and local products like olive oil and wine as souvenirs.

Majorca is a versatile destination that caters to a wide range of travelers. Whether you're seeking relaxation on pristine beaches, adventure in the mountains, or cultural exploration in historic towns, Majorca has something to offer. With its pleasant climate, stunning landscapes, and rich heritage, this Mediterranean gem should be on every traveler's bucket list. Explore, experience, and create lasting memories in Majorca.

• Why Visit Majorca

Majorca, the largest of Spain's Balearic Islands, is a destination that has captivated travelers for decades. With its stunning landscapes, rich history, vibrant culture, and diverse activities, Majorca offers an unforgettable experience for all types of visitors. In this comprehensive travel guide, we will delve into the reasons why you should make Majorca your next travel destination.

1. Breathtaking Beaches

One of the primary draws of Majorca is its incredible beaches. The island boasts over 200 beaches with crystal-clear waters and soft golden sands. Whether you prefer a lively beach with water sports and beach bars or a secluded cove for a tranquil escape, Majorca has it all. Among the must-visit beaches are Playa de Muro, Cala Agulla, and Es Trenc.

2. Stunning Natural Beauty

Majorca's landscapes are nothing short of spectacular. The island's interior is characterized by rugged mountains, lush valleys, and charming villages. The Tramuntana Mountain Range, a UNESCO World Heritage Site, is a hiker's paradise, offering challenging trails and breathtaking vistas. Don't miss the opportunity to explore the Serra de Tramuntana, which stretches along the northwest coast.

3. Historic Palma de Mallorca

The capital city, Palma de Mallorca, is a vibrant blend of history and modernity. The historic old town, known as La Seu, features narrow cobblestone streets, Gothic architecture, and a stunning cathedral that dominates the skyline. Explore the Almudaina Palace, stroll through the lively squares, and indulge in tapas at local restaurants.

4. Cultural Experiences

Majorca's cultural scene is rich and diverse. Throughout the year, the island hosts various festivals, music events, and art exhibitions.

Traditional celebrations like the Sant Joan Festival and the Moors and Christians Festival provide a glimpse into Majorca's heritage. Visit the Fundació Pilar i Joan Miró to admire the works of the famous artist Joan Miró, who lived on the island.

5. Water Activities

Majorca's crystal-clear waters are perfect for a wide range of water activities. Scuba diving enthusiasts can explore underwater caves and vibrant marine life. Sailing and windsurfing are popular options, and you can rent equipment or take lessons at numerous coastal locations. For a more relaxed experience, go snorkeling in the pristine coves.

6. Gastronomic Delights

The island's cuisine is a delightful blend of Mediterranean flavors. Try the local seafood dishes like paella and tumbet, or savor a traditional sobrassada sausage. Majorca is also known for its excellent wines, so be sure to visit a vineyard for a tasting. The vibrant markets, such as Mercat de l'Olivar in Palma, offer fresh produce and local specialties.

7. Family-Friendly Destination

Majorca is a fantastic destination for families. Many resorts and hotels cater specifically to families with children, offering kid-friendly amenities and activities. The island's beaches are safe for swimming, and you can explore family-friendly attractions like the Palma Aquarium, Katmandu Park, and Marineland.

8. Nightlife and Entertainment

Majorca comes alive after dark with a bustling nightlife scene. Palma offers a wide range of bars, clubs, and music venues. The Paseo Marítimo area is known for its vibrant nightlife, where you can dance the night away. For a more relaxed evening, enjoy a cocktail at a beachfront bar and savor the Mediterranean breeze.

9. Charming Villages

While Palma is the capital, Majorca is also dotted with charming villages that offer an authentic taste of island life. Sóller, with its quaint tram and scenic gardens, is a favorite among tourists. Valldemossa, a picturesque hillside village, is famous for its monastery and the composer Frédéric Chopin, who once lived there.

10. Wellness and Relaxation

Majorca is a haven for wellness seekers. The island boasts numerous spa resorts and wellness retreats set against stunning natural backdrops. Whether you're looking for yoga and meditation retreats or luxurious spa treatments, Majorca has plenty to offer in terms of relaxation and rejuvenation.

11. Diverse Accommodation Options

Majorca offers a wide range of accommodation options to suit every budget and preference. From luxury beachfront resorts to cozy boutique hotels and charming countryside villas, you can find the perfect place to stay for your vacation.

12. Accessibility

Getting to Majorca is convenient, with Palma de Mallorca Airport serving as the main gateway. Many European cities offer direct flights to the island, making it easily accessible for travelers from around the world.

13. Year-Round Destination

Majorca enjoys a Mediterranean climate, which means it's a year-round destination. Whether you prefer the warm summer months for beach activities or the mild winters for hiking and exploring, Majorca has something to offer no matter when you visit.

Majorca, with its breathtaking beaches, stunning landscapes, rich history, and vibrant culture, is a destination that caters to every traveler's desires. Whether you seek relaxation, adventure, or a mix of both, this Balearic gem has it all. Majorca invites you to explore its diverse offerings, creating memories that will last a lifetime. Plan your trip to Majorca, and let this island paradise enchant you with its beauty and charm.

•Getting to Majorca

Mallorca, also known as Majorca, is a picturesque island located in the Mediterranean Sea. It's part of the Balearic Islands, which also include Ibiza, Menorca, and

Formentera. Majorca is renowned for its stunning landscapes, beautiful beaches, vibrant culture, and rich history. Whether you're a nature enthusiast, a beach lover, or a history buff, Majorca has something to offer everyone. In this comprehensive travel guide, we will explore how to get to Majorca and provide you with all the essential information you need for a memorable trip to this enchanting island.

Getting to Majorca

1.1. Choosing Your Travel Dates

Before you start planning your trip to Majorca, it's essential to decide on your travel dates. Majorca enjoys a Mediterranean climate, with hot, dry summers and mild, wet winters. The peak tourist season is during the summer months, from June to August, when the weather is warm and sunny. However, if you prefer a quieter and more budget-friendly experience, consider visiting during the shoulder seasons of spring (March to May) or autumn (September to November).

1.2. Selecting Your Transportation

Getting to Majorca is relatively straightforward, thanks to its well-connected transportation network. You have several options for reaching the island:

a. By Air: Palma de Mallorca Airport (PMI) is the main gateway to Majorca and one of Spain's busiest airports. It receives flights from major cities in Europe and beyond. Airlines like Ryanair, easyJet, and Lufthansa offer direct flights to Majorca from various destinations.

b. By Sea: If you prefer a more scenic route, you can take a ferry to Majorca. Ferries operate from mainland Spain, including Barcelona and Valencia, as well as from other Mediterranean ports. The journey by sea offers breathtaking views of the coastline as you approach the island.

c. Cruises: Majorca is a popular stop for Mediterranean cruises. Many cruise lines include the island in their itineraries, allowing you to explore the island's beauty for a day during your cruise.

1.3. Booking Your Flights or Ferry

Once you've decided on your mode of transportation, it's time to book your tickets. To get the best deals, consider booking your flights or ferry tickets well in advance, especially if you plan to travel during the peak season. Comparison websites and travel agencies can help you find the most affordable options.

1.4. Travel Documents and Visa

Before traveling to Majorca, make sure you have all the necessary travel documents. If you are an EU or EFTA (European Free Trade Association) citizen, you can enter Majorca with just a valid passport or national ID card. However, if you're from a non-EU country, check the Spanish government's official website for visa requirements.

Arriving in Palma de Mallorca

2.1. Palma de Mallorca Airport

Upon arriving at Palma de Mallorca Airport, you'll find yourself on the island's southwest coast. This airport is conveniently located, making it easy to access various parts of the island. The airport offers car rental services, taxis, and shuttle buses to help you reach your accommodation.

2.2. Transportation from the Airport

a. Taxis: Taxis are readily available at the airport and are a convenient way to reach your destination. Ensure that the taxi has a meter, and the driver uses it, or agree on a fixed price before starting your journey.

b. Airport Shuttle Buses: Airport shuttle buses connect the airport with popular tourist destinations across Majorca. They are a cost-effective option for getting to your hotel.

c. Car Rentals: If you plan to explore the island extensively, renting a car at the airport can be a great option. Majorca has well-maintained roads, and a rental car gives you the flexibility to visit less accessible places.

2.3. Accommodation in Palma

Palma, the capital city of Majorca, is a popular place to stay for many travelers. It offers a wide range of accommodation options, from luxury hotels to budget-friendly hostels. Popular areas to stay in Palma include the Old Town (La

Lonja), Santa Catalina, and Portixol. Make sure to book your accommodation in advance, especially during the peak season.

Getting Around Majorca

3.1. Public Transportation

Majorca has a reliable and extensive public transportation system, making it easy to explore the island without a car. The main modes of public transport include buses and trains. The TIB (Transport Illes Balears) network connects different towns and attractions, and you can purchase tickets at stations or on board.

3.2. Renting a Bicycle

For eco-conscious travelers and those who enjoy cycling, Majorca offers numerous opportunities to rent bicycles. The island has a network of bike lanes and scenic routes, allowing you to explore its beauty at a leisurely pace.

3.3. Renting a Scooter or Motorcycle

Renting a scooter or motorcycle can be a fun and convenient way to explore Majorca, especially if you want to reach more remote areas. However, ensure you have the necessary license and follow local traffic rules.

3.4. Driving in Majorca

If you decide to rent a car, be aware that driving in Majorca is on the right side of the road. Familiarize yourself with local traffic regulations, and make sure your rental car has proper insurance coverage. Parking can be challenging in busy areas, so plan accordingly.

CHAPTER TWO

Planning Your Trip

•*Best Time to Visit*

Majorca, the largest of the Balearic Islands in Spain, offers a Mediterranean paradise for travelers. To make the most of your visit, it's essential to choose the right time to go. Here's a breakdown of the best times to experience Majorca's beauty:

Spring (March to May): Spring is a delightful season to explore Majorca. The weather is mild, with temperatures ranging from 15°C to 22°C (59°F to 72°F). The island's lush landscapes come to life with colorful blooms, making it perfect for nature enthusiasts and hikers.

Summer (June to August): Summer is peak tourist season, thanks to its warm temperatures ranging from 25°C to 31°C (77°F to 88°F). Beach lovers will relish the crystal-clear waters, while partygoers can enjoy the vibrant nightlife. However, be prepared for larger crowds and higher prices.

Autumn (September to November): If you prefer a quieter visit but still desire pleasant weather, consider autumn. Temperatures hover around 20°C to 26°C (68°F to 79°F). You can enjoy the beaches without the summer crowds and explore the island's cultural attractions.

Winter (December to February): Majorca remains relatively mild during the winter, with temperatures averaging 10°C to 15°C (50°F to 59°F). While it's not ideal for swimming, winter is perfect for a peaceful getaway. You can explore historic towns, visit museums, and enjoy local cuisine without the summer hustle.

The best time to visit Majorca depends on your preferences. Whether you seek vibrant summer energy or a serene winter escape, Majorca has something to offer year-round. Plan your trip accordingly to make the most of this Mediterranean gem.

• Visa and Entry Requirements

Majorca, also known as Mallorca, is a beautiful island in the Mediterranean Sea and a popular tourist destination. To ensure a smooth and hassle-free trip, it's crucial to understand the visa and entry requirements for visiting Majorca.

Visa Exemptions

Schengen Area: Majorca is a part of the Schengen Area, which allows citizens of Schengen member countries to enter without a visa for short stays (usually up to 90 days within a 180-day period).

European Union: Citizens of European Union (EU) countries can travel to Majorca using their national ID card or passport, with no need for a visa.

Visa Requirements

Non-Schengen Citizens: If you're not a citizen of a Schengen country or an EU member state, you may need a Schengen visa to enter Majorca for tourism purposes. Check with the Spanish embassy or consulate in your country for specific requirements and application procedures.

Visa Application Process: Typically, you will need to apply for a Schengen visa at the Spanish embassy or consulate nearest to your place of residence. The application process may require you to provide proof of travel, accommodation reservations, financial means, and travel insurance.

Length of Stay

Short-Stay Visas: Schengen visas for Majorca are typically issued for short stays, usually up to 90 days within a 180-day period. Be sure to plan your trip within these limits.
Passport Requirements

Valid Passport: Ensure your passport is valid for at least six months beyond your planned departure date from Majorca. It's a standard requirement for most international travel.

Blank Visa Pages: Check that your passport has enough blank visa pages for entry and exit stamps.

Entry and Exit

Entry Stamp: Upon arrival in Majorca, make sure to get an entry stamp on your passport.

This indicates your date of entry, which is important for complying with the 90-day limit.

Exit Stamp: When leaving Majorca, ensure you receive an exit stamp. This is proof of your departure and can be important for future visa applications.

Visa Extensions

Extending Your Stay: If you wish to extend your stay in Majorca beyond the allowed 90 days, you may need to apply for an extension through the Spanish immigration authorities. This process can be complex, so it's advisable to consult with local immigration offices for guidance.

Travel Insurance

Mandatory Insurance: While not a strict visa requirement, it's highly recommended to have travel insurance when visiting Majorca. This insurance should cover medical emergencies, trip cancellations, and other unforeseen events. Additional Considerations

COVID-19 Restrictions: Depending on the current situation, Majorca may have specific

COVID-19 related entry requirements, such as testing and vaccination certificates. Always check the latest travel advisories and entry requirements before your trip.

Customs Regulations: Familiarize yourself with the customs regulations of Majorca and Spain to avoid any issues when bringing in or taking out items such as alcohol, tobacco, or souvenirs.

Local Laws and Regulations: Be aware of and respect local laws and regulations in Majorca, including those related to behavior, photography, and cultural sensitivities.

Visiting Majorca can be an incredible experience, but it's essential to understand and meet the visa and entry requirements to ensure a stress-free journey. Remember to check for the most up-to-date information and consult with the appropriate authorities or travel agencies for guidance on your specific situation. By planning ahead and adhering to the necessary regulations, you can fully enjoy the beauty and culture that Majorca has to offer.

• *Accommodation Options*

Majorca, the largest of Spain's Balearic Islands, is a Mediterranean paradise known for its stunning landscapes, rich history, and vibrant culture. Whether you're planning a relaxing beach getaway, an adventure-filled holiday, or a cultural exploration, choosing the right accommodation is essential to make the most of your trip. In this comprehensive travel guide, we'll explore the diverse range of accommodation options that Majorca offers, catering to various budgets, preferences, and travel styles.

1. *Luxury Resorts and Hotels:*

Majorca boasts a plethora of luxurious resorts and hotels, especially in areas like Palma de Mallorca, Port de Pollença, and Cala d'Or. These establishments offer world-class amenities, breathtaking sea views, and top-notch service. Consider options like the Belmond La Residencia in Deià or the St. Regis Mardavall Mallorca Resort in Costa d'en Blanes for an opulent experience.

2. *Boutique Hotels:*

For travelers seeking a more intimate and unique atmosphere, boutique hotels in Majorca are an excellent choice. These charming properties often feature distinctive designs, personalized service, and a strong sense of local character. Explore places like Can Bordoy Grand House & Garden in Palma or Hotel Posada Terra Santa for an authentic Majorcan experience.

3. Vacation Rentals and Villas:
If you prefer independence and space, vacation rentals and villas provide a home-away-from-home experience. Majorca offers a wide range of options, from quaint countryside cottages to luxurious beachfront villas. Websites like Airbnb and Vrbo have listings throughout the island, allowing you to choose the perfect setting for your stay.

4. Budget-Friendly Hotels and Hostels:
Travelers on a budget need not worry, as Majorca also offers numerous affordable accommodation options. Hostels in Palma and other towns are ideal for backpackers and solo travelers. Additionally, budget-friendly hotels and guesthouses provide comfortable stays without breaking the bank.

5. Agroturismos:
For a unique and rustic experience, consider staying at an agroturismo. These are traditional

Majorcan farmhouses that have been converted into charming guesthouses. You'll have the chance to immerse yourself in rural life while enjoying modern comforts.

6. All-Inclusive Resorts:
Majorca is home to several all-inclusive resorts that cater to families and travelers looking for hassle-free vacations. These resorts often include meals, activities, and entertainment in their packages, making them a convenient choice for those who want an all-encompassing experience.

7. Glamping and Eco-Lodges:
For eco-conscious travelers and nature enthusiasts, glamping sites and eco-lodges provide a sustainable and immersive way to experience the island's natural beauty. These accommodations often prioritize environmental conservation and offer unique stays in the midst of nature.

8. Camping:
For the ultimate outdoor adventure, camping in Majorca's national parks and natural reserves is a fantastic option. Be sure to check the regulations and obtain necessary permits if you plan to camp in protected areas.

9. Timeshares and Vacation Clubs:
Some visitors may opt for timeshare properties or vacation clubs, which offer a combination of flexibility and amenities. If you're a member of such a program, Majorca may have affiliated properties to consider.

10. Unconventional Stays:
Majorca also has a range of unconventional accommodations, including treehouses, cave hotels, and even lighthouses turned into lodging. These options promise a memorable and one-of-a-kind experience.

•Budgeting for Your Trip
Majorca, a beautiful Mediterranean island belonging to Spain, is a popular tourist destination known for its stunning beaches, vibrant nightlife, and rich cultural heritage. Whether you're planning a relaxing beach vacation or an adventurous exploration of the island's natural beauty, budgeting for your trip is crucial to ensure you make the most of your experience without breaking the bank. In this guide, we'll walk you through various aspects of budgeting for your trip to Majorca.

1. Establishing Your Budget

The first step in budgeting for your Majorca trip is determining how much you can afford to spend. Consider your total available funds and the duration of your stay. Break down your budget into categories such as accommodation, transportation, food, activities, and miscellaneous expenses. This will help you allocate funds appropriately and avoid overspending.

2. Flights and Transportation

a. Booking Flights

Start by researching flight options to Majorca. Prices can vary significantly depending on the time of year and your departure location. Be flexible with your travel dates, as flying during the off-peak season can result in substantial savings. Additionally, consider using flight comparison websites and signing up for fare alerts to find the best deals.

b. Local Transportation

Majorca has a well-developed public transportation system, including buses and trams. Purchase a transport pass or card if you plan to use public transport frequently during your stay. Alternatively, renting a bicycle or scooter can be a cost-effective way to explore the island independently.

3. Accommodation
a. Types of Accommodation

Majorca offers a range of accommodation options, from luxury resorts to budget-friendly hostels and vacation rentals. Choose accommodation that aligns with your budget. Booking in advance can often secure better rates. Additionally, consider staying in less touristy areas for lower prices.

b. Alternative Accommodation

If you're open to unique experiences, explore options like camping or glamping. Majorca has beautiful natural settings that are perfect for camping enthusiasts. Just be sure to check local regulations and obtain necessary permits.

4. Dining
a. Eating Out

Majorca boasts a diverse culinary scene, with options to suit various budgets. To save money, opt for local eateries and street food stalls, which often offer delicious and affordable meals. Avoid dining in tourist-heavy areas where prices can be inflated.

b. Self-Catering
If you have access to a kitchen in your accommodation, consider buying groceries from local markets and cooking your meals. This can be a significant money-saver, especially for families or those on extended trips.

5. Activities and Entertainment
Majorca offers a wealth of activities, from beach days to cultural tours. To stay within your budget:

a. Prioritize Activities
Select a few must-do activities and plan your budget around them. Research free or low-cost attractions, such as hiking trails and public beaches, to fill your itinerary without overspending.

b. Discount Cards and Packages
Look for tourist cards or packages that offer discounted access to multiple attractions. These can provide substantial savings if you plan to visit several museums, landmarks, or theme parks.

6. Miscellaneous Expenses

Don't forget to budget for unexpected or miscellaneous expenses. This category can include souvenirs, travel insurance, and emergency funds. Setting aside a small portion of your budget for these expenses will help you handle any surprises without stress.

7. Currency Exchange and Payment Methods
Before your trip, research the local currency and exchange rates. It's often wise to carry a mix of cash and cards for different situations. Notify your bank of your travel plans to avoid any issues with card usage abroad.

Budgeting for your trip to Majorca is essential to ensure you have a memorable and financially stress-free experience. By carefully planning and allocating your funds to various aspects of your trip, you can make the most of this beautiful Mediterranean destination without breaking the bank. Remember to stay flexible, explore cost-saving options, and savor the unique experiences Majorca has to offer within your budget. Enjoy your trip!

CHAPTER THREE

Exploring Majorca

•*Major Cities and Regions*

Majorca, often spelled Mallorca, is one of Spain's most enchanting islands, nestled in the sparkling waters of the Mediterranean Sea. This Balearic gem is renowned for its stunning beaches, rich history, vibrant culture, and picturesque landscapes. In this travel guide, we'll take you on a journey through Majorca, exploring its major cities and regions, uncovering the hidden gems, and providing you with all the essential information to make your visit unforgettable.

I. Palma de Mallorca - The Capital City:
Palma de Mallorca, commonly referred to as Palma, is the capital city and the gateway to the island. It's a bustling hub of culture, history, and entertainment. Here are some must-visit attractions in Palma:

La Seu Cathedral: This magnificent Gothic cathedral is an architectural marvel that overlooks the sea. Its interior boasts intricate stained glass windows and a serene atmosphere.

Bellver Castle: A circular fortress perched on a hill, Bellver Castle offers panoramic views of Palma and its surroundings. It's a great spot for history buffs and photographers.

Palma Old Town: Wander through the narrow, winding streets of the old town, where you'll find charming cafes, boutiques, and historic buildings.

Es Baluard Museum: Art enthusiasts should not miss this contemporary art museum, featuring works by local and international artists.

II. Serra de Tramuntana - The Mountain Range:

The Serra de Tramuntana is a UNESCO World Heritage Site that stretches across the northwest coast of Majorca. This rugged and scenic region is perfect for nature lovers and hikers. Highlights include:

Hiking Trails: Explore numerous hiking trails that lead you through picturesque villages like

Valldemossa and Deià. The views of the coastline and mountains are breathtaking.

Sa Calobra: A winding road takes you to this stunning cove with crystal-clear waters. It's a great spot for swimming and relaxation.

Fornalutx: This charming village is often considered one of Spain's most beautiful. Stroll through its stone streets and admire the well-preserved architecture.

III. East Coast - Beach Paradise:
The east coast of Majorca is famous for its beautiful beaches and crystal-clear waters. Some notable places to visit in this region include:

Cala d'Or: A resort town known for its sandy coves and upscale hotels. Enjoy a relaxing day at Cala Gran or Cala Mondragó.

Caves of Drach: These limestone caves are a natural wonder with underground lakes. Visitors can take a boat ride while listening to classical music concerts.

Porto Cristo: A charming fishing village where you can explore its marina and dine at seafood restaurants along the waterfront.

IV. North Coast - Hidden Gems:
The northern coast of Majorca is less crowded and offers a more tranquil experience. Explore:

Pollença: A picturesque town with a vibrant Sunday market and the iconic Calvary Steps, offering panoramic views.

Alcúdia: Known for its historic old town surrounded by medieval walls and stunning beaches.

Formentor Peninsula: A stunning natural area with a lighthouse, beautiful beaches, and breathtaking viewpoints.

V. Inland Majorca - Rustic Charm:
Venture into the heart of the island to discover its rustic charm and traditional way of life. Highlights include:

Sineu: Visit its weekly market, one of the oldest on the island, and enjoy authentic local produce and crafts.

Es Pla Region: This agricultural heartland boasts vineyards, almond orchards, and picturesque villages like Petra and Sencelles.

Bodegas and Wine Tasting: Majorca produces excellent wines, and many vineyards welcome visitors for tastings and tours.

Majorca is a diverse island that offers something for every traveler. Whether you're seeking the vibrant city life of Palma, the natural beauty of the Serra de Tramuntana, the tranquil beaches of the east coast, the hidden gems of the north, or the rustic charm of the inland regions, Majorca promises an unforgettable experience. So, pack your bags, immerse yourself in the Mediterranean culture, and let Majorca enchant you with its beauty and hospitality. Enjoy your journey!

• *Top Attractions*

Mallorca, often referred to as Majorca, is a gem in the Mediterranean Sea and one of Spain's most beloved destinations. With its stunning beaches, rich history, vibrant culture, and natural beauty, this Balearic Island has something for every traveler. In this guide, we will take you on a journey through the top attractions and experiences that await you in Majorca.

I. Palma de Mallorca: The Capital City

Palma Cathedral (La Seu)
The iconic Palma Cathedral, with its Gothic architecture, is a must-visit. Its stunning rose window and interior design are awe-inspiring.

Almudaina Palace
Explore the historic Almudaina Palace, a symbol of the island's royal history, and enjoy panoramic views of the city from its terraces.

Es Baluard Museum of Modern and Contemporary Art
Art enthusiasts will appreciate Es Baluard's impressive collection of modern and contemporary art, housed within a unique fortress-like building.

Old Town (La Lonja and Sa Gerreria)
Wander through the charming streets of the Old Town, where you'll find quaint shops, tapas bars, and a vibrant atmosphere.

II. Beaches and Coastlines

Playa de Muro
Relax on the pristine Playa de Muro, known for its crystal-clear waters and soft white sands, perfect for sunbathing and water sports.

Cala Varques
For a more secluded beach experience, venture to Cala Varques, a hidden gem accessible only by foot or boat. It offers tranquility and natural beauty.

Sa Calobra
Discover the dramatic beauty of Sa Calobra, a stunning cove surrounded by cliffs and accessible via a winding road, perfect for scenic drives.

III. Natural Wonders

Tramuntana Mountains
Hike or drive through the UNESCO-listed Tramuntana Mountains, offering breathtaking views, charming villages, and opportunities for outdoor adventures.

Caves of Drach (Cuevas del Drach)
Explore the magical underground world of the Caves of Drach, complete with underground

lakes and a mesmerizing classical music concert.

IV. Charming Villages

Valldemossa
Visit the picturesque village of Valldemossa, known for its narrow streets, historic monastery, and the famous composer Frederic Chopin.

Deià
Deià, another charming village, is a haven for artists and writers, with its stunning sea views and cultural heritage.

V. Culinary Delights

Tapas and Paella
Indulge in traditional Spanish dishes, including tapas and paella, at local restaurants and beachfront cafés.

Local Markets
Explore the bustling markets in towns like Sineu or Inca, where you can taste local cheeses, olives, and fresh produce.

VI. Outdoor Activities

Cycling
Majorca is a popular destination for cycling enthusiasts, with its scenic routes and pleasant climate. Rent a bike and explore the island's beauty.

Water Sports
Enjoy a variety of water sports, such as snorkeling, scuba diving, and sailing, at the island's numerous beaches and marinas.

VII. Festivals and Events

Fiesta de Sant Joan
Experience the lively Fiesta de Sant Joan in June, celebrated with bonfires, fireworks, and music throughout the island.

Semana Santa
Witness the religious traditions of Semana Santa (Holy Week) with processions and ceremonies in Palma.

VIII. Accommodation

Luxury Resorts

Majorca offers a range of luxury resorts, such as Belmond La Residencia in Deià, providing world-class amenities and stunning views.

Boutique Hotels
For a unique and intimate experience, stay in charming boutique hotels scattered across the island.

IX. Transportation

Car Rental
Renting a car is the best way to explore Majorca's hidden treasures and remote villages.

Public Transportation
The island also has an efficient bus and train network, making it easy to navigate without a car.

This guide provides an overview of Majorca's top attractions, but the island has so much more to offer. Whether you're seeking relaxation, adventure, culture, or cuisine, Majorca welcomes you with open arms. Plan your trip, embrace the island's diverse offerings, and create unforgettable memories in this Mediterranean paradise.

Beaches and Coastal   Destinations

Majorca, the largest of Spain's Balearic Islands, is renowned for its stunning beaches and picturesque coastal landscapes. This travel guide will take you on a journey to some of the island's most alluring coastal destinations, offering sun-soaked adventures and tranquil escapes.

1. Palma de Mallorca: Gateway to the Island

Begin your Majorca adventure in Palma de Mallorca, the capital city. While it's not primarily a beach destination, Palma boasts a beautiful seafront promenade, Paseo Marítimo, perfect for leisurely strolls. Visit Palma Cathedral, a stunning Gothic masterpiece, and explore the historic Old Town with its charming narrow streets.

2. Playa de Palma: Urban Beach Bliss

A short drive from Palma, you'll find Playa de Palma. This bustling beach is known for its golden sands and vibrant atmosphere. It's lined with restaurants, bars, and water sports facilities, making it a fantastic spot for both relaxation and entertainment.

3. Cala Millor: Family-Friendly Fun

For a family-friendly beach experience, head to Cala Millor on the eastern coast. Its shallow, clear waters are ideal for swimming, and the promenade is dotted with shops and restaurants. A picturesque lighthouse overlooks the bay, adding to the charm.

4. Cala d'Or: Cove-Hopping Paradise

Cala d'Or is a resort town known for its unique coastline of small coves and bays. Cala Gran and Cala Esmeralda are among the most popular. These intimate settings are perfect for snorkeling and sunbathing. The town itself offers a delightful Mediterranean ambiance with its whitewashed buildings and lush gardens.

5. Cala Figuera: A Fishing Village Gem

Experience the authentic side of Majorca in Cala Figuera, a quaint fishing village. While it doesn't have a sandy beach, its natural harbor, dotted with colorful boats, is a picturesque setting for a leisurely afternoon. Enjoy fresh seafood at one of the waterfront restaurants.

6. Sóller and Port de Sóller: Tram Ride to Paradise

Sóller, nestled in the Tramuntana Mountains, can be reached by a historic wooden tram. The charming town is a gateway to Port de Sóller, a coastal village with a horseshoe-shaped bay. Stroll along the promenade, savor the local citrus fruits, and take in the stunning scenery.

7. Sa Calobra: Dramatic Beauty

For a dose of dramatic coastal beauty, venture to Sa Calobra. This secluded spot boasts turquoise waters, rugged cliffs, and the mesmerizing Torrent de Pareis gorge. Accessible by boat or a winding mountain road, it's a must-visit for nature enthusiasts.

8. Formentor Peninsula: Nature's Paradise

The Formentor Peninsula, in the north of the island, offers a natural paradise. Visit Cap de Formentor for breathtaking views and discover hidden coves like Cala Murta and Cala Figuera. The scenic drive through the pine-clad mountains is an adventure in itself.

9. Magaluf: Vibrant Nightlife

If you're looking for a vibrant nightlife scene, Magaluf is the place to be. During the day, relax on the sandy beaches, and when the sun sets, enjoy the lively bars and clubs. It's a hotspot for party-goers.

10. Cala Mondragó: Pristine Nature Reserve

End your coastal journey at Cala Mondragó, a protected nature reserve in the southeast. This beach is surrounded by pine forests and dunes, offering a tranquil escape from the crowds. It's an excellent spot for birdwatching and hiking.

Majorca's beaches and coastal destinations cater to a wide range of travelers, from families seeking relaxation to adventurers in search of natural beauty. With its diverse offerings, this island in the Mediterranean is a true gem for beach lovers and explorers alike. Make the most of your Majorca vacation by exploring its stunning coastlines and enjoying the warm Mediterranean sun.

Historical Sites

Palma Cathedral (La Seu):
Palma Cathedral is an architectural masterpiece that dates back to the 13th century. Its stunning Gothic design and intricate interior make it one of Majorca's most iconic landmarks. Visitors can explore its magnificent rose window, the Royal Chapel, and the Miquel Barceló's contemporary art installations.

Bellver Castle:
This circular castle, built in the 14th century, is a unique example of Gothic architecture. It offers panoramic views of Palma and its harbor. The castle also houses the City History Museum, providing insight into the island's past.

Alcudia Old Town:
The old town of Alcudia is enclosed within well-preserved medieval walls. It's a charming place to wander through narrow streets, visit

the local market, and explore historical sites like the Roman ruins of Pollentia.

Valldemossa:
Valldemossa is a picturesque village known for its charming streets, historic buildings, and the Royal Carthusian Monastery. This monastery, where composer Frédéric Chopin once stayed, offers a glimpse into the island's cultural heritage.

Santuari de Lluc:
Nestled in the Tramuntana Mountains, this religious sanctuary dates back to the 13th century. It's a significant pilgrimage site and offers a tranquil retreat for visitors interested in Majorca's spiritual history.

Ses Païsses:
Located near Arta, Ses Païsses is an ancient Talaiotic settlement dating back to the Bronze Age. Explore the prehistoric ruins and learn about the island's early inhabitants.

Capdepera Castle:
This medieval fortress overlooks the town of Capdepera and offers spectacular views of the surrounding countryside. The castle has a rich

history and is well-preserved, making it a great spot for history enthusiasts.

Sa Dragonera:

This uninhabited island off the coast of Majorca has historical significance as a former pirate hideout. Today, it's a nature reserve where visitors can hike and explore the island's rugged terrain.

Museu de Mallorca:

Located in Palma, this museum houses a vast collection of art and artifacts, showcasing Majorca's history and culture. It's a great place to gain a deeper understanding of the island's heritage.

Archaeological Sites:

Majorca boasts various archaeological sites, including ancient Roman ruins and talaiots (prehistoric stone structures). These sites offer a glimpse into the island's diverse history.

When visiting these historical sites in Majorca, it's essential to respect their cultural and historical significance. Take your time to soak in the rich heritage of the island, and don't forget to enjoy the stunning natural beauty and Mediterranean cuisine that Majorca has to offer as well. This diverse blend of history, culture, and natural beauty makes Majorca a fantastic destination for travelers seeking a well-rounded experience.

Natural Parks

Majorca, the largest of Spain's Balearic Islands, is renowned for its stunning beaches, vibrant culture, and rich history. However, beyond the bustling resorts and lively nightlife, Majorca hides a natural treasure trove waiting to be explored. The island is home to several beautiful natural parks that offer a tranquil escape from the crowds and a chance to connect with nature. In this comprehensive travel guide, we will take you on a journey through the natural parks of Majorca, revealing their unique beauty and the experiences they offer.

1. S'Albufera Natural Park
Location: Northern Majorca, near Alcúdia

S'Albufera Natural Park is a sprawling wetland paradise, making it one of the most important wetlands in the Balearic Islands. This park is a haven for birdwatchers and nature enthusiasts, boasting over 200 species of birds, including herons, flamingos, and ospreys.

What to Do:
Birdwatching: Grab your binoculars and spot unique avian species in their natural habitat.
Hiking and Cycling: Explore the park's trails by foot or bike, meandering through reed beds and lush landscapes.
Boat Tours: Take a boat ride through the canals to get a different perspective of the park's beauty.
Insider Tip:
Visit during the early morning or late afternoon for the best birdwatching experiences when many species are most active.

2.   *Cabrera   Archipelago Maritime-Terrestrial National Park*
Location: Southeast of Majorca, accessible via boat from Colònia de Sant Jordi

Cabrera Archipelago is a hidden gem, consisting of 19 islands and islets. This national park is a protected marine and terrestrial area, home to diverse flora and fauna.

What to Do:

Boat Excursions: Embark on a boat trip to explore the islands' pristine waters, marine life, and historic sites.

Snorkeling and Diving: Dive into the crystal-clear waters to discover underwater caves and vibrant marine ecosystems.

Hiking: Trek the island of Cabrera itself to appreciate its natural beauty and historical sites.

Insider Tip:

Since visitor numbers are limited daily, be sure to book your boat tour in advance to secure your spot.

3. Mondragó Natural Park

Location: Southeast Majorca, near Santanyí

Mondragó Natural Park is a picturesque coastal reserve famous for its pristine beaches, dramatic cliffs, and lush pine forests. It's a haven for beach lovers and hikers alike.

What to Do:

Beach Relaxation: Sunbathe on Mondragó's beautiful beaches, such as S'Amarador and Cala Mondragó.

Hiking Trails: Explore the park's trails through pine groves and coastal cliffs, offering breathtaking vistas.

Picnicking: Enjoy a picnic surrounded by nature in designated areas.
Insider Tip:
Arrive early to secure a parking spot, especially during the peak tourist season, as this park can get quite crowded.

4. Dragonera Natural Park
Location: West of Majorca, accessible by boat from Sant Elm

Dragonera Island, named for its dragon-like shape, is a protected natural park with rugged landscapes, sea caves, and a rich history.

What to Do:
Hiking: Trek across the island on well-marked trails to viewpoints with panoramic sea views.
Visit the Lighthouse: Explore the iconic lighthouse at the island's tip and learn about its maritime history.
Boat Tours: Take a boat tour to explore the sea caves and discover the island's marine life.
Insider Tip:
Pack comfortable hiking shoes and plenty of water, as some trails can be challenging.

5. Sierra de Tramuntana

Location: Northwestern Majorca, stretching along the island's spine

The Sierra de Tramuntana is a UNESCO World Heritage-listed mountain range known for its dramatic landscapes, charming villages, and historic trails.

What to Do:
Hiking: Embark on the famous GR-221 hiking route, covering the length of the Sierra de Tramuntana.
Village Exploration: Visit picturesque villages like Valldemossa, Sóller, and Fornalutx.
Cycling: Enjoy cycling through scenic mountain roads with breathtaking views.
Insider Tip:
Visit in spring or autumn for pleasant weather and fewer tourists, as summer can be quite hot for hiking.

6. Albufereta Natural Park
Location: Northeastern Majorca, near Can Picafort

Albufereta Natural Park is a smaller sibling of S'Albufera, offering a quieter and more intimate natural experience. It's perfect for those seeking tranquility.

What to Do:

Nature Walks: Stroll along the wooden walkways and enjoy the peaceful atmosphere.

Birdwatching: Spot various bird species in this coastal wetland.

Photography: Capture the park's serene beauty and its reflections in the calm waters.

Insider Tip:

Bring insect repellent, especially during the warmer months, to protect yourself from mosquitoes.

7. Cala d'Or Marine Natural Park

Location: Southeastern Majorca, near Cala d'Or

Cala d'Or Marine Natural Park is a coastal paradise known for its crystalline waters, sea caves, and underwater wonders.

What to Do:

Snorkeling and Scuba Diving: Explore the park's marine life and caves beneath the surface.

Boat Tours: Take a boat excursion to visit secluded coves and hidden beaches.

Kayaking: Paddle along the picturesque coastline to discover hidden gems.

Insider Tip:
Rent snorkeling gear in advance or bring your own to fully enjoy the underwater beauty.

8. Llevant Peninsula Natural Park
Location: Eastern Majorca, near Artà

Llevant Peninsula Natural Park offers a diverse landscape of rugged cliffs, hidden coves, and dense forests, making it a paradise for outdoor enthusiasts.

What to Do:
Hiking: Discover the park's trails, including the challenging ascent to the Talaia de Son Jaumell, a rewarding viewpoint.
Beach Hopping: Explore pristine beaches like Cala Torta and Cala Mitjana for a relaxing day by the sea.
Wildlife Watching: Keep an eye out for rare species like the Balearic lizard and the black vulture.
Insider Tip:
Check trail conditions before hiking, as some paths may be closed due to maintenance or fire risk.

9. Montserrat Natural Park
Location: Western Majorca, near Valldemossa

Montserrat Natural Park is a hidden gem nestled in the Tramuntana mountains, known for its mystical caves and ancient monastic history.

What to Do:
Cave Exploration: Visit the Cova de Sant Aniol, a stunning cave with underground lakes.
Monastery Visit: Explore the historical Valldemossa Charterhouse, where Chopin and George Sand famously stayed.
Scenic Drives: Enjoy picturesque drives through the mountains, with viewpoints offering breathtaking vistas.
Insider Tip:
Be prepared for narrow, winding mountain roads when driving to the park, and consider taking a guided tour for cave exploration.

10. Sa Dragonera Natural Park
Location: Off the west coast of Majorca, accessible by boat from Sant Elm

Sa Dragonera is a small island natural park, famous for its rugged cliffs, lighthouses, and unique flora and fauna.

What to Do:

Hiking: Explore the island's trails, leading to stunning viewpoints and the iconic Dragonera Lighthouse.

Birdwatching: Spot local and migratory bird species, including Eleonora's falcon.

Historical Sites: Visit ancient watchtowers and learn about the island's history.

Insider Tip:

Combine a visit to Sa Dragonera with a boat tour to discover the surrounding marine life.

Majorca's natural parks offer a diverse range of experiences for nature lovers, outdoor enthusiasts, and anyone seeking a break from the bustling tourist areas. Whether you're interested in hiking, birdwatching, snorkeling, or simply relaxing on pristine beaches, Majorca's natural parks have something to offer. Plan your visit to these hidden gems and immerse yourself in the island's natural beauty, making your trip to Majorca truly unforgettable.

Cultural Experiences

Majorca, the largest of Spain's Balearic Islands, is a captivating destination that offers a rich tapestry of cultural experiences for travelers. From its stunning Mediterranean landscapes to its vibrant local traditions, this Majorca travel guide will delve deep into the island's cultural heritage, exploring its history, cuisine, festivals, and more.

1. Historical Heritage

Majorca's history is a blend of various cultures, making it a treasure trove of historical sites. Palma, the capital city, is home to the imposing Palma Cathedral, a masterpiece of Gothic architecture. Visitors can explore the Almudaina Palace, a stunning royal residence dating back to the Middle Ages, and wander through the narrow streets of the Old Town, where medieval buildings and quaint squares await.

2. Art and Museums

Majorca boasts an impressive art scene. The Fundació Joan Miró, dedicated to the renowned Catalan artist, houses an extensive collection of his works. The Es Baluard Museum of Modern and Contemporary Art is another must-visit, showcasing local and international artists. Additionally, Palma's historic buildings often serve as galleries, providing art enthusiasts with a unique cultural experience.

3. Local Cuisine

Food plays a significant role in any culture, and Majorca is no exception. The island's cuisine is a delightful blend of Mediterranean flavors with a local twist. Sample traditional dishes like "paella de mariscos" (seafood paella), "sobrassada" (spicy sausage), and "ensaimada" (a sweet, coiled pastry). Don't forget to pair your meal with a glass of locally produced wine or "pomada," a gin and lemonade cocktail.

4. Festivals and Celebrations

Majorca hosts a wide range of festivals throughout the year, offering a glimpse into its vibrant culture. The Sant Sebastià Festival in January, the Easter processions, and the Sant Joan Festival in June are just a few examples. During these celebrations, locals and visitors come together to enjoy music, dance, and fireworks, creating a lively atmosphere.

5. Traditional Crafts

Exploring Majorca's traditional crafts is a unique way to connect with the local culture. The island is known for its handmade products, including intricate pottery, delicate glassware, and exquisite pearls. Visitors can watch skilled artisans at work in various workshops and even purchase these locally crafted souvenirs.

6. Language and Traditions

The official languages in Majorca are Catalan and Spanish, but many locals also speak English and German due to tourism. Learning a few basic Catalan phrases can enhance your cultural experience and help you connect with the people of Majorca. Additionally, understanding local customs and traditions, such as the "dimoni" (devil) figures in festivals or the "talaiots" (prehistoric megalithic structures), can provide valuable insights into the island's heritage.

7. Nature and Landscape

Majorca's natural beauty is intertwined with its cultural heritage. The rugged Tramuntana Mountains, a UNESCO World Heritage site, offer breathtaking vistas and hiking opportunities. The picturesque coastline with its hidden coves and crystal-clear waters is a testament to the island's natural allure. Nature lovers can explore the S'Albufera Natural Park, a haven for birdwatchers and wildlife enthusiasts.

8. Music and Dance

Music and dance are integral to Majorca's cultural fabric. Traditional music includes the "xeremies" (bagpipes) and "castanets" played during folkloric performances. Flamenco, while not originally from Majorca, has also found a home here, with regular performances showcasing passionate guitar playing and mesmerizing dance routines.

9. Religious Heritage

Majorca has a rich religious heritage, evident in its many churches and monasteries. The Lluc Monastery, nestled in the Tramuntana Mountains, is a significant pilgrimage site and houses the beloved "La Moreneta" statue. The Sanctuary of Sant Salvador in Felanitx offers panoramic views of the island, making it a spiritual and scenic attraction.

10. Outdoor Markets

Exploring the local markets is an excellent way to immerse yourself in Majorca's culture. The Mercat de l'Olivar in Palma is a bustling food market where you can savor fresh produce, seafood, and regional specialties. Additionally, the weekly street markets in towns across the island provide opportunities to shop for artisanal goods and interact with locals.

11. Ethnological Museums

Ethnological museums like the Museu Etnològic de Mallorca offer a deeper understanding of the island's traditions and way of life. These museums showcase everything from traditional clothing and tools to recreations of old Majorcan homes, providing an insightful journey into the island's history and culture.

12. Water Sports and Maritime Heritage

Given its coastal location, Majorca has a strong maritime tradition. Visitors can engage in water sports such as sailing, snorkeling, and windsurfing while learning about the island's maritime history. The Maritime Museum in

Palma provides a fascinating look into Majorca's seafaring past.

13. Sustainability and Conservation

In recent years, Majorca has made significant efforts to preserve its cultural and natural heritage. Sustainable tourism practices, such as protecting the Posidonia seagrass meadows and promoting eco-friendly transportation, are vital to preserving the island's unique environment and culture for future generations to enjoy.

14. Rural Life and Agritourism

Venturing into Majorca's rural areas allows travelers to experience the island's agricultural traditions firsthand. Agritourism options offer a chance to stay on working farms, participate in activities like olive picking, and taste farm-fresh products, giving insight into the agrarian culture of Majorca.

15. Connectivity and Accessibility

Majorca is well-connected, with an international airport in Palma de Mallorca serving as the main gateway to the island. Once on Majorca, public transportation and rental cars make it easy to explore various cultural sites and attractions.

Majorca's cultural experiences are as diverse as its landscapes, offering something for every traveler. Whether you're interested in history, cuisine, art, or outdoor adventures, this Balearic gem invites you to immerse yourself in its rich heritage. As you explore the island's historical sites, indulge in its culinary delights, and participate in local traditions, you'll find that Majorca is a cultural tapestry waiting to be discovered.

•Outdoor Activities

Majorca, the largest of the Balearic Islands in the Mediterranean Sea, is a paradise for outdoor enthusiasts. With its stunning landscapes, diverse ecosystems, and favorable climate, Majorca offers a wide range of outdoor activities for nature lovers and adventure seekers. In this travel guide, we'll delve into the top outdoor activities you can enjoy while visiting this beautiful island.

Hiking in the Tramuntana Mountains

The Tramuntana Mountains, a UNESCO World Heritage site, are a must-visit for hikers. Stretching along the northwest coast of Majorca, these rugged peaks offer a plethora of trails for hikers of all levels. The GR 221, also known as the Dry Stone Route, is a famous long-distance trail that spans the entire mountain range. It offers breathtaking views of the coastline and the chance to explore charming mountain villages like Sóller and Fornalutx.

For a more challenging adventure, tackle the Puig Major, the island's highest peak. The hike to its summit promises unmatched vistas of the surrounding landscapes. Be sure to check the weather conditions and come prepared with appropriate gear, as the weather in the mountains can be unpredictable.

Cycling and Mountain Biking

Majorca is a cyclist's paradise, known for its well-maintained roads and diverse terrain. Whether you're a road cyclist or a mountain biker, you'll find plenty of opportunities to explore the island on two wheels. The flat plains in the south and the winding mountain roads in the north offer something for everyone.

The picturesque coastal roads are perfect for leisurely bike rides, while the challenging mountain trails in the Tramuntana Mountains provide an adrenaline rush for mountain biking enthusiasts. Many bike rental shops are available across the island, and you can even join guided cycling tours if you prefer a structured experience.

Water Sports and Beach Activities

With its crystal-clear waters and numerous beaches, Majorca is a water sports haven. Try your hand at windsurfing, kitesurfing, or stand-up paddleboarding at popular beaches like Playa de Palma and Alcúdia. For a more relaxed experience, go snorkeling or scuba diving to explore the vibrant underwater world teeming with marine life.

Majorca also offers excellent conditions for sailing and boating. Charter a boat and cruise along the coast, stopping at secluded coves and beaches that are only accessible by sea. The island's marinas are well-equipped to accommodate boaters and sailors.

Rock Climbing and Deep-Water Soloing

For rock climbing enthusiasts, Majorca boasts some world-class climbing spots, especially along the dramatic cliffs of the coast. Deep-water soloing is a unique experience where climbers ascend rock faces directly above the sea, with no ropes or harnesses. The clear waters below provide a thrilling cushion for those daring enough to take on the challenge.

Cala Barques in Cala Santanyí and Es Pontàs in Santanyí are famous deep-water soloing locations. If you're into traditional rock climbing, explore the limestone crags in the interior of the island, such as the Cova del Diablo near Alcúdia.

Golfing in Paradise

Majorca offers several world-class golf courses with stunning views of the Mediterranean Sea and the Tramuntana Mountains. The island's golf clubs welcome players of all skill levels. Some notable golf courses include Golf de

Andratx, Golf Santa Ponsa, and Alcanada Golf Club. Tee off amidst the lush greenery and enjoy a relaxing game in the Mediterranean sunshine.

Exploring Caves and Coves

Majorca is home to a network of mesmerizing caves, and exploring them is an adventure in itself. The Caves of Drach (Cuevas del Drach) and the Caves of Artà (Cuevas de Artà) are the most famous. These underground wonders feature stunning stalactites and stalagmites formations, as well as subterranean lakes where you can enjoy classical music concerts in the Caves of Drach.

The island's coastline is dotted with picturesque coves, many of which are accessible only by boat or on foot. Cala Pi, Cala Figuera, and Cala Varques are some hidden gems that offer tranquility and natural beauty away from the bustling tourist areas.

Bird Watching and Nature Reserves

Majorca's diverse landscapes are home to a rich variety of bird species, making it a fantastic destination for bird watchers. The Albufera

Natural Park, located near Alcúdia, is a significant wetland area that attracts migratory birds. Grab your binoculars and explore the park's trails to spot herons, flamingos, and other avian species.

Stargazing in Remote Locations

Escape the light pollution of the cities and head to remote locations in the Tramuntana Mountains for an unforgettable stargazing experience. Majorca's clear skies and low levels of light pollution make it an ideal spot for astronomy enthusiasts. You can even join astronomy tours organized by local experts to get a deeper understanding of the night sky.

Tips for Outdoor Activities in Majorca

Weather: Majorca enjoys a Mediterranean climate with hot, dry summers and mild winters. Plan your outdoor activities accordingly, and always check the weather forecast before heading out.

Safety: Safety should be a priority. If you're engaging in adventurous activities like hiking, biking, or climbing, ensure you have the necessary equipment and knowledge. It's also a good idea to inform someone about your plans and expected return time.

Respect Nature: Respect the environment and local regulations. Leave no trace, and preserve the natural beauty of the island for future generations.

Local Guidance: Consider hiring local guides or joining guided tours, especially for activities like rock climbing or exploring caves. They can provide valuable insights and ensure your safety.

Majorca is a paradise for outdoor enthusiasts, offering a wide range of activities that cater to all interests and skill levels. From hiking in the Tramuntana Mountains to cycling along scenic coastal roads, and from diving into crystal-clear waters to exploring enchanting caves, Majorca has it all. So, pack your outdoor gear and immerse yourself in the natural wonders of this Mediterranean jewel. Your adventure awaits on the stunning island of Majorca!

Hiking and Biking

Majorca, also known as Mallorca, is a jewel in the Mediterranean, offering travelers a diverse range of experiences, from pristine beaches to historic towns. But for those seeking an active and immersive outdoor adventure, hiking and biking in Majorca are unparalleled. In this comprehensive travel guide, we will delve into the island's picturesque trails and biking routes, providing you with all the information you need to embark on an unforgettable outdoor journey.

Hiking in Majorca

The Terrain
Majorca's terrain is a hiker's paradise. With its rugged mountains, dramatic cliffs, lush valleys, and pristine beaches, the island offers a wide variety of hiking experiences. The Tramuntana mountain range, a UNESCO World Heritage site, is a prime destination for hikers. The trails here wind through olive groves, pine forests, and terraced farms, providing breathtaking vistas of the sea and neighboring islands.

Must-Visit Hiking Routes
a. GR 221 - The Dry Stone Route

The GR 221, also known as the Dry Stone Route, is a long-distance trail that crosses the Tramuntana range from Andratx in the southwest to Pollença in the northeast. This challenging but rewarding hike showcases Majorca's natural beauty and traditional dry-stone architecture. Along the way, you can explore charming villages like Sóller and Deià.

b. Torrent de Pareis
For a more adventurous hike, the Torrent de Pareis is a must. It takes you through a spectacular canyon with towering cliffs and crystal-clear water. This route is not for the faint of heart, but the views are well worth the effort.

c. Cap de Formentor
If you prefer coastal walks, head to Cap de Formentor, located at the northeastern tip of the island. This route offers panoramic views of the rugged coastline and the Mediterranean Sea.

Hiking Tips
Wear appropriate hiking shoes and clothing, as some trails can be rocky and uneven.
Carry plenty of water, especially during the hot summer months.

Check trail conditions and weather forecasts before setting out, and consider guided tours if you're unfamiliar with the terrain.

Cultural Highlights

Hiking in Majorca isn't just about the natural beauty; it's also an opportunity to explore the island's rich history and culture. Visit monasteries like Lluc and Valldemossa, both nestled in the Tramuntana mountains, to learn about Majorca's religious heritage and enjoy stunning architecture.

Biking in Majorca

Cycling Paradise

Majorca has earned its reputation as a cycling paradise, attracting cyclists from around the world. The island's diverse terrain and excellent road infrastructure make it an ideal destination for bikers of all levels, from beginners to professional athletes.

Road Cycling

a. Serra de Tramuntana Loop

The Serra de Tramuntana mountain range offers some of the best road cycling in Europe. A popular route is the challenging Serra de Tramuntana loop, which takes you through hairpin bends and climbs with breathtaking views.

b. Coastal Routes

For a more leisurely ride, explore the coastal roads that wind along the Mediterranean, passing through charming fishing villages and picturesque beaches.

Mountain Biking

If you prefer off-road adventures, Majorca has an array of mountain biking trails suitable for all skill levels. The hilly terrain of the Tramuntana mountains offers exciting downhill descents and technical trails.

Cycling Tips

Renting a bike is easy in Majorca, with numerous rental shops catering to various types of bicycles.
Ensure your bike is in good condition, and carry essential tools for repairs.
Respect traffic rules and be mindful of other road users.

Biking Events

Majorca hosts various cycling events throughout the year, including the Mallorca 312, a challenging sportive that circumnavigates the island, and the Mallorca Classic, attracting professional cyclists. Participating in these events can add an extra layer of excitement to your biking experience.

Practical Information

Best Time to Visit
The optimal time for hiking and biking in Majorca is spring (April to June) and early autumn (September to October). During these periods, the weather is pleasant, and the trails are less crowded.

Accommodation
Majorca offers a range of accommodations, from luxury resorts to charming boutique hotels and budget-friendly hostels. Many establishments cater specifically to outdoor enthusiasts and cyclists, offering bike storage and maintenance facilities.

Transportation
Getting around Majorca is relatively easy. Renting a car is a popular option, but you can also use public buses to access hiking trails and cycling routes. Additionally, some areas offer bike-friendly transportation, such as bike rental shops and cycling tour operators.

Safety

Safety should always be a top priority when engaging in outdoor activities. Inform someone of your hiking or biking plans, carry a map or GPS device, and be prepared for emergencies with basic first aid supplies.

Hiking and biking in Majorca are experiences that allow you to connect with nature, explore stunning landscapes, and immerse yourself in the island's rich culture. Whether you're seeking a challenging adventure or a leisurely ride along the coast, Majorca has something to offer every outdoor enthusiast. So, pack your hiking boots or hop on your bike, and get ready to discover the beauty of Majorca through these thrilling outdoor activities. Your unforgettable journey awaits on this Mediterranean gem.

Water Sports

Majorca, the largest of Spain's Balearic Islands, is renowned for its stunning landscapes, pristine beaches, and vibrant culture. While the island has much to offer in terms of relaxation and sightseeing, it's also a water sports enthusiast's paradise. In this Majorca travel guide, we will delve into the thrilling world of water sports on this beautiful island, highlighting the diverse range of activities available for both beginners and seasoned adventurers.

Introduction to Majorca's Water Sports Scene

Majorca's Mediterranean location blesses it with warm waters, gentle breezes, and a diverse coastline that is perfect for water sports of all kinds. Whether you're seeking the adrenaline rush of jet skiing, the serenity of paddleboarding, or the excitement of windsurfing, Majorca has something for everyone.

Jet Skiing: Riding the Waves

For those looking to add a dash of excitement to their beach vacation, jet skiing in Majorca is a thrilling option. Jet ski rentals are readily available at various beaches, and no prior experience is required. You'll receive a brief lesson on operating the jet ski safely, and then you're off to explore the crystal-clear waters of the Mediterranean. Zoom along the coast, feeling the wind in your hair and the spray of the sea on your face as you ride the waves.

Windsurfing: Harnessing the Breeze

Majorca's consistent sea breezes make it a windsurfer's paradise. With numerous windsurfing schools scattered along the coast, beginners can easily get started. More experienced windsurfers can bring their own equipment or rent from local shops. The Bay of Pollensa and Playa de Palma are particularly popular spots due to their reliable wind conditions and stunning backdrops of mountains and beaches.

Sailing: Navigating the Mediterranean

Sailing enthusiasts will find Majorca to be a dream destination. Whether you're an experienced sailor or a beginner, there are opportunities to charter boats or join group tours. Explore secluded coves, hidden beaches, and charming coastal villages as you sail the Mediterranean. Many tours even offer the chance to anchor in a tranquil bay for swimming and snorkeling.

Scuba Diving: Exploring the Underwater World

Majorca boasts a rich underwater world waiting to be explored. The island's clear waters are teeming with marine life and feature intriguing underwater caves and rock formations. Dive centers are plentiful, and both beginners and experienced divers can take guided dives. Cabrera National Park, a protected marine area, offers some of the most spectacular diving experiences in the Mediterranean.

Snorkeling: A Window to the Sea

For those who prefer to stay closer to the surface, snorkeling in Majorca provides an opportunity to witness the island's underwater beauty. All you need is a mask, snorkel, and fins to start your adventure. Snorkeling is easily accessible from the shore, and you can explore colorful fish and vibrant coral reefs. Cala Figuera and Cala d'Or are popular snorkeling spots with calm, clear waters.

Paddleboarding: Serenity on the Surface

Paddleboarding has become increasingly popular in Majorca due to its simplicity and versatility. It's a fantastic way to explore the coastline at your own pace. Whether you want to take a leisurely paddle along the shore or venture into sea caves, paddleboarding offers a serene and unique perspective of Majorca's beauty. Many beaches offer paddleboard rentals, and guided tours are also available.

Kitesurfing: Riding the Wind and Waves

Kitesurfing combines elements of windsurfing and wakeboarding, offering an exhilarating experience for thrill-seekers. Majorca's windy conditions make it an ideal destination for kitesurfing. Experienced kitesurfers can bring their own equipment, while beginners can take lessons at various kitesurfing schools along the coast. Alcudia and Can Pastilla are popular kitesurfing spots.

Wakeboarding: Riding the Wake

For those who enjoy the rush of being towed behind a speedboat, wakeboarding is an exciting water sport in Majorca. Whether you're a beginner or an experienced rider, you can find wakeboarding centers offering lessons and rentals. Glide across the water and perform impressive tricks as you're pulled by the boat, all while enjoying the beautiful coastal scenery.

Fishing: A Leisurely Pursuit

Fishing enthusiasts will find Majorca to be an excellent destination for angling. The island offers various fishing experiences, from deep-sea fishing to fishing from the shore. Charter a fishing boat and try your luck at catching a variety of species, including tuna, swordfish, and dorado. Alternatively, you can cast your line from the tranquil beaches and rocky shores.

Kayaking: Exploring Coastal Wonders

Kayaking is a fantastic way to explore Majorca's rugged coastline and hidden coves. Rent a kayak or join a guided tour to paddle along the crystal-clear waters. You can access secluded beaches that are often unreachable by land and take in the breathtaking scenery. The calm waters of Alcudia Bay and the dramatic cliffs of Cala Sant Vicenç are ideal kayaking destinations.

Majorca's water sports scene offers a diverse range of activities that cater to adventurers of all levels. Whether you seek the adrenaline rush of jet skiing, the tranquility of paddleboarding, or the exploration of scuba diving, Majorca has it all. With its stunning coastline, warm Mediterranean waters, and a myriad of water sports centers, Majorca is the ultimate destination for outdoor enthusiasts looking to make a splash in the sea. So, pack your swimwear and sunscreen, and get ready to embark on an unforgettable aquatic adventure on this beautiful Balearic Island.

Golfing

Nestled in the serene beauty of the Mediterranean, Majorca, also known as Mallorca, offers an idyllic setting for outdoor enthusiasts. Among the many activities that the island has to offer, golfing stands out as a premier choice. In this Majorca travel guide, we will explore the enchanting world of golfing in Majorca, delving into its history, the top golf courses, the perfect golfing weather, and how to make the most of your golfing experience on this enchanting island.

A Brief History of Golfing in Majorca

Golfing in Majorca has a rich history that dates back to the early 20th century. The Royal Bendinat Golf Club, founded in 1986, is one of the oldest golf clubs on the island. Originally designed by Martin Hawtree, this 18-hole course offers stunning views of the Mediterranean Sea, making it a must-visit for golf enthusiasts.

Majorca's golfing scene started to gain prominence in the 1990s when several high-quality golf courses were built. The island's favorable climate, with mild winters and sunny summers, contributed to its popularity among golfers from around the world. Over the years, Majorca has become a premier destination for golfers seeking a perfect blend of challenging courses and natural beauty.

Top Golf Courses in Majorca

Majorca boasts a plethora of world-class golf courses that cater to players of all skill levels. Whether you're a seasoned pro or a beginner looking to learn, you'll find a course that suits your needs. Here are some of the top golf courses on the island:

Son Gual Golf: Designed by Thomas Himmel, this course is renowned for its immaculate condition and challenging layout. The picturesque views of the Tramuntana Mountains make it a golfer's paradise.

Golf de Andratx: Located in Camp de Mar, this Robert Trent Jones Jr. masterpiece features stunning sea views and dramatic elevation changes. Its diverse layout offers an exciting challenge for golfers of all abilities.

Golf Alcanada: Situated in Alcudia, this course is famous for its unique design that incorporates the natural terrain and boasts spectacular views of Alcudia Bay. The lighthouse overlooking the course adds to the charm.

Pula Golf: A classic course with a rich history, Pula Golf in Son Servera was designed by José Maria Olazábal. It offers a combination of woodland and parkland holes, making it a diverse and enjoyable experience.

Real Golf de Bendinat: As one of the oldest golf courses on the island, it has a classic design and offers panoramic views of the

Mediterranean Sea. Its charming clubhouse adds to the overall experience.

Maioris Golf: Located near Palma, this course is known for its modern design and challenging layout. It's a great option for golfers looking for a convenient course near the capital.

Santa Ponsa Golf: With three 18-hole courses to choose from, Santa Ponsa Golf Club provides variety and beautiful surroundings. It's a popular choice for golfers of all levels.

Perfect Golfing Weather

Majorca's Mediterranean climate is a significant draw for golfers. The island experiences long, sunny summers and mild winters, creating ideal conditions for year-round golfing. The peak golfing season typically runs from March to November when the weather is warm and dry, making it perfect for tee times and post-round relaxation on the terrace of the clubhouse.

During the summer months, temperatures can reach the mid-30s°C (mid-90s°F), so early morning or late afternoon tee times are recommended to avoid the heat. In contrast, the mild winters are perfect for those looking for a golfing escape from colder climates, with daytime temperatures averaging around 15-20°C (59-68°F).

Making the Most of Your Golfing Experience

To make the most of your golfing experience in Majorca, consider these tips:

Book Tee Times in Advance: Majorca's golf courses can get busy, especially during the peak season. Booking your tee times well in advance ensures you get the slots you prefer.

Stay at Golf Resorts: Many resorts on the island offer golf packages that include accommodation and access to nearby courses. It's a convenient way to combine leisure and golf.

Explore the Island: While golfing is a highlight, don't forget to explore Majorca's other attractions. The island is known for its stunning beaches, historic towns, and beautiful landscapes.

Dine at Clubhouses: Clubhouses at golf courses often feature excellent restaurants. Enjoy a post-round meal with views of the course and the Mediterranean.

Pack Accordingly: Depending on the season, pack appropriate golf attire and sunscreen. The Mediterranean sun can be strong, so protecting yourself from UV rays is essential.

Golfing in Majorca is a captivating outdoor activity that combines the thrill of the sport with the beauty of the Mediterranean landscape. With a rich history of golf, a variety of top-notch courses, and favorable weather conditions, Majorca has rightfully earned its reputation as a premier golfing destination. Whether you're a golf enthusiast or a novice looking to try something new, Majorca's golf courses await, promising an unforgettable experience in this paradise on Earth.

•Shopping and Dining

Majorca, the jewel of the Mediterranean, is a destination that offers not only pristine beaches and stunning landscapes but also a vibrant culture deeply rooted in its shopping and dining experiences. In this Majorca travel guide, we'll delve into the world of outdoor shopping and dining on this beautiful island, exploring the unique blend of traditional and modern elements that make it a paradise for tourists seeking to savor both local flavors and retail therapy under the sun.

Outdoor Shopping in Majorca

Markets Galore:

Majorca boasts a plethora of open-air markets that cater to every taste. The most famous of these is the Sineu Market, held every Wednesday. It's not just a shopping destination but a vibrant social event where locals and tourists mingle. From fresh produce to handmade crafts, clothing, and even livestock, Sineu Market is a sensory feast.

Artisanal Treasures:

In the heart of Palma, you'll find the Artà Market, a showcase of artisanal craftsmanship. Here, you can pick up unique souvenirs such as pottery, leather goods, and jewelry. Strolling through the stalls, you'll witness local artisans honing their craft, giving you a glimpse into Majorca's artistic heritage.

Luxury Shopping:

For those seeking high-end fashion and luxury items, the swanky streets of Palma, such as Passeig des Born and Avinguda Jaume III, are the go-to destinations. Exclusive boutiques featuring renowned designers, as well as international brands, line these avenues, making it a haven for fashion enthusiasts.

Local Markets:

For a more authentic experience, explore the smaller local markets found in villages and towns throughout the island. These markets offer a chance to discover local products and connect with the warm-hearted Majorcan people. You might stumble upon olive oil, wines, cheeses, and other culinary delights that Majorca is known for.

Outdoor Dining in Majorca

Al Fresco Dining:

Dining outdoors is a cherished tradition in Majorca. Many restaurants and cafes offer delightful terraces where you can savor your meals while enjoying the island's pleasant climate. Whether you're in Palma, on the coast, or nestled in the countryside, al fresco dining is an integral part of the Majorcan experience.

Mediterranean Cuisine:

Majorca's cuisine is heavily influenced by its Mediterranean location. You'll find a delightful array of seafood dishes featuring fresh catches from the surrounding waters. Try "paella," a rice dish infused with local flavors, or "sobrassada," a delicious cured sausage unique to the island.

Tapas Culture:

Tapas are a beloved Spanish tradition, and Majorca is no exception. Many restaurants and bars offer tapas menus, allowing you to sample a variety of small, flavorful dishes. Pair them with a glass of local wine or a refreshing "sangria" for the ultimate culinary experience.

Rural Retreats:

In the rural areas of Majorca, you'll discover hidden gems where dining feels like a retreat into nature. Finca restaurants, set amidst olive groves or vineyards, serve dishes made from locally sourced ingredients. These rustic settings offer a peaceful escape from the hustle and bustle of city life.

The Fusion of Shopping and Dining

One of the unique aspects of Majorca is how shopping and dining often intertwine. Many markets have food stalls where you can taste local delicacies while you shop. For example, the Santa Catalina Market in Palma is not only a place to buy fresh produce but also a hotspot for foodies, offering a wide variety of gourmet delights.

Additionally, some restaurants partner with local artisans to create a holistic experience. You might find a restaurant that serves dishes on handmade ceramics from a nearby pottery shop or one that pairs its cuisine with wines from a neighboring vineyard. These experiences showcase the island's commitment to preserving its traditions while embracing modern influences.

A Sustainable Approach

Majorca is increasingly adopting sustainable practices in both shopping and dining. From farmers' markets that promote locally grown, organic produce to restaurants sourcing ingredients from nearby farms, the island is making strides towards a more eco-conscious approach to gastronomy and commerce.

Majorca offers a rich tapestry of outdoor shopping and dining experiences that cater to all tastes and preferences. Whether you're wandering through bustling markets, indulging in Mediterranean delicacies at a seaside restaurant, or exploring the countryside's rustic charm, Majorca's outdoor activities are sure to leave you with lasting memories of this enchanting island. Embrace the fusion of tradition and modernity, savor the flavors of the Mediterranean, and immerse yourself in the vibrant culture of Majorca as you explore its outdoor shopping and dining scene.

CHAPTER FOUR

Travel Tips

• *Local Cuisine and Food Specialities*

Mallorca, the largest of Spain's Balearic Islands, is not only renowned for its stunning beaches, picturesque landscapes, and vibrant culture but also for its rich and diverse culinary traditions. The island's cuisine is a delightful fusion of Spanish, Mediterranean, and even Moorish influences, making it a paradise for food lovers. In this Majorca travel guide, we'll take you on a gastronomic journey through the island, highlighting its local cuisine and food specialties.

Traditional Dishes:

A. Paella: While paella is often associated with mainland Spain, it has a prominent place in Mallorca's culinary repertoire. The island's version, known as "Arroz Brut," is a hearty rice dish cooked with saffron, vegetables, and a variety of meats, typically rabbit or chicken. The unique twist lies in the use of rich local olive oil and the strong flavors of garlic and paprika.

B. Sobrassada: Mallorca's famous cured sausage, sobrassada, is a must-try for any visitor. Made from ground pork, paprika, and other spices, it's often spread on warm bread or used as an ingredient in various dishes. The island also hosts an annual Sobrassada Fair, celebrating this delectable sausage.

C. Tumbet: Tumbet is a vegetarian delight, composed of layers of fried potatoes, red bell peppers, aubergines, and tomatoes, drizzled with olive oil and seasoned with garlic and herbs. It's a comforting and flavorsome dish that showcases the island's fresh produce.

Seafood Extravaganza:
Given its coastal location, Mallorca is a seafood lover's paradise. Fresh catches from the Mediterranean Sea feature prominently in local cuisine. Here are some seafood specialties to savor:

A. Caldereta de Langosta: This rich and flavorful lobster stew is a true delicacy. Prepared with lobster, tomatoes, onions, garlic, and a touch of brandy, it's a dish reserved for special occasions.

B. Gambas a la Plancha: Grilled prawns, seasoned with olive oil, garlic, and sea salt, are a simple yet delicious treat that highlights the natural flavors of the sea.

C. Soller Prawns: The picturesque town of Soller is famous for its succulent prawns. They are often prepared with a hint of lemon and olive oil to let the prawns' sweetness shine through.

Unique Breads:
Mallorca boasts a variety of bread types that are integral to its cuisine. One of the most famous is "Pan Morena," a dense, dark bread made with whole wheat flour, seeds, and nuts, creating a hearty and nutritious option.

Local Cheeses:
Mallorca is home to several artisanal cheese producers, crafting unique varieties that reflect the island's terroir. Try "Mahon" cheese, a semi-hard cow's milk cheese with a tangy flavor, or "Torta," a creamy and soft sheep's milk cheese perfect for spreading on bread.

Desserts and Pastries:

Mallorca's sweet treats are a delightful way to end a meal. Be sure to indulge in:

A. Ensaimada: This spiral-shaped pastry, dusted with powdered sugar, is a beloved Mallorcan dessert. It can be enjoyed plain or filled with cream, chocolate, or even apricot jam.

B. Crespells: These delicate, star-shaped cookies are flavored with anise and make for a delightful snack alongside a cup of coffee.

C. Almond-based treats: Mallorca is famous for its almond groves, and almonds find their way into many desserts. Don't miss "Gató," a moist almond cake, or "Turrón," a nougat made with almonds and honey.

Local Markets:

To truly immerse yourself in Mallorca's food culture, visit the local markets. Palma's Mercat de l'Olivar is a bustling hub of fresh produce, seafood, meats, and regional specialties. It's a sensory delight with vibrant colors, enticing aromas, and friendly vendors.

Wine and Spirits:

Mallorca also has a budding wine industry, with vineyards producing unique varietals. Be sure to taste the local wines, such as the crisp white "Prensal Blanc" and the red "Manto Negro." Additionally, sample the island's herbal liqueur, "Hierbas," which is often enjoyed as a digestive after a meal.

Dining Experiences:
Mallorca offers a range of dining experiences to suit every palate and budget. From beachfront chiringuitos serving fresh seafood to Michelin-starred restaurants showcasing innovative Mediterranean cuisine, you're spoiled for choice.

A. Beachfront Dining: Enjoy a seafood feast at one of the many beachside restaurants where you can dine with your toes in the sand.

B. Traditional Mallorcan Restaurants: Seek out family-run restaurants that specialize in traditional Mallorcan dishes for an authentic culinary experience.

C. Fine Dining: For a special occasion, book a table at one of the island's upscale eateries, where renowned chefs create culinary masterpieces.

Food Festivals:

If your visit coincides with one of Mallorca's food festivals, you're in for a treat. Some notable events include:

A. Fira del Pebre Bord: This festival celebrates the local red pepper, "pebre bord," with cooking demonstrations, tastings, and live music.

B. Fira del Vi: Wine enthusiasts will delight in this wine fair, featuring local wineries and tastings of the island's best vintages.

Mallorca is not just a destination for sun and sea; it's a culinary paradise waiting to be explored. The island's rich history and diverse cultural influences have given rise to a vibrant food scene that's both traditional and innovative. From savory paellas to sweet ensaimadas, Mallorcan cuisine has something to satisfy every palate. So, when you visit this beautiful island, don't forget to indulge in its local cuisine and food specialties – it's an integral part of the Mallorcan experience.

• *Language and Communication*

Majorca, the largest of the Balearic Islands, is a breathtaking Mediterranean destination known for its stunning landscapes, vibrant culture, and warm hospitality. While the island's natural beauty and historical sites are sure to captivate any traveler, effective language and communication play a crucial role in enhancing your experience on this enchanting island. In this comprehensive Majorca travel guide, we will explore the importance of language and communication, providing you with essential information to make the most of your visit.

The Languages of Majorca

Majorca is a diverse and culturally rich destination, and this diversity is reflected in the languages spoken on the island. The two primary languages are Spanish and Catalan. Here's an overview of each:

Spanish: As Majorca is part of Spain, Spanish, or "Castilian," is the official language. The majority of locals, especially those in the service industry and tourist areas, are proficient in Spanish. If you are well-versed in

Spanish, you'll have no trouble communicating with most residents.

Catalan: Catalan is the co-official language of Majorca and holds cultural significance for the islanders. While many locals speak Catalan, especially in more rural areas, you'll find that most also speak Spanish. It's worth noting that Catalan can differ slightly from the standard Spanish you may be familiar with.

English is widely spoken in tourist areas, hotels, restaurants, and shops. You'll also encounter other European languages, such as German and French, due to the island's popularity among European tourists.

Language Tips for Travelers

Learn Basic Phrases: While English is prevalent, making an effort to learn some basic Spanish and Catalan phrases can go a long way in bridging cultural gaps and showing respect to the locals. Simple greetings like "Hola" (Hello) and "Gracias" (Thank you) can make a positive impression.

Use Translation Apps: Technology has made it easier than ever to communicate in foreign countries. Download translation apps to help with language barriers, but don't solely rely on them. Learning a few essential phrases is a great way to connect with locals.

Politeness Matters: Politeness is universal. Be courteous, patient, and respectful when communicating with locals. A friendly attitude can often transcend language barriers.

Smile and Gestures: Non-verbal communication, such as smiling and using gestures, can convey a lot of meaning. If you're struggling to find the right words, a warm smile can help bridge the gap.

Ask for Help: Don't hesitate to ask for help when needed. Most Majorcans are friendly and willing to assist tourists, especially if you approach them politely.

Menu Understanding: When dining out, it's helpful to understand menu items. Familiarize yourself with common Spanish and Catalan food terms to make ordering easier.

Cultural Sensitivity

Understanding the culture of Majorca is just as important as language when it comes to communication. Majorca has a rich history and traditions, and being culturally sensitive can greatly enhance your travel experience. Here are some cultural tips to keep in mind:

Respect Local Customs: Majorcans take pride in their traditions. Be mindful of local customs and festivals. If you're visiting during a celebration, join in the festivities respectfully.

Dress Code: When visiting churches or more conservative areas, consider dressing modestly. It's a sign of respect for the culture and religion.

Tipping: Tipping is customary in Majorca, and it's appreciated. In restaurants, leaving a tip of around 10% is typical.

Siesta Time: Keep in mind that many shops and businesses in Majorca observe the siesta, a midday break. Plan your activities accordingly, as some places may close during this time.

Punctuality: Majorcans value punctuality, so make an effort to arrive on time for appointments or reservations.

Greeting Customs: Greetings in Majorca are often warm and friendly. A handshake or kiss on both cheeks is common when meeting someone.

Exploring Majorca

Now that you're equipped with language and cultural knowledge, let's delve into the diverse experiences Majorca offers:

Beaches: Majorca boasts some of the most beautiful beaches in the Mediterranean. Whether you prefer the bustling Playa de Palma or the secluded Cala Varques, the island has a beach for every taste.

Historical Sites: Explore the island's rich history by visiting sites like the Palma Cathedral, Bellver Castle, and the ancient ruins of Pollentia. Guided tours are available in multiple languages.

Natural Beauty: Discover Majorca's natural wonders by hiking in the Serra de Tramuntana mountains or exploring the caves of Drach. Local guides can enhance your experience with informative commentary.

Local Cuisine: Savor the island's gastronomic delights, including paella, ensaimada (a sweet pastry), and fresh seafood. Don't miss the opportunity to try local wines and traditional dishes.

Festivals: Majorca hosts numerous festivals throughout the year, celebrating its culture and heritage. The Fira de la Llampuga in Porto Cristo and the Sant Sebastià Festival in Palma are just a couple of examples.

Outdoor Activities: From water sports to cycling, Majorca offers a wide range of outdoor activities. Many tour operators provide services in various languages.

Shopping: Explore local markets and boutique stores to find unique souvenirs. Bargaining is not common in Majorca, so be prepared to pay the listed prices.

Majorca is a remarkable destination that offers a blend of natural beauty, rich culture, and warm hospitality. Effective language and communication skills will undoubtedly enhance your experience on this stunning island. By learning a few basic phrases, respecting local customs, and approaching your interactions with openness and respect, you'll be well-prepared to explore all that Majorca has to offer. Whether you're lounging on its pristine beaches, savoring its delectable cuisine, or immersing yourself in its vibrant culture, Majorca is sure to leave you with cherished memories that last a lifetime.

• *Transportation within Majorca*

Majorca, also known as Mallorca, is a stunning Spanish island located in the Mediterranean Sea. Known for its picturesque landscapes, beautiful beaches, and rich cultural heritage, Majorca is a top tourist destination. To fully explore and enjoy this island, it's crucial to understand the various transportation options available. In this comprehensive travel guide, we will delve into the intricate network of transportation within Majorca, ranging from buses and trains to taxis and car rentals.

Air Travel:

Majorca is well-connected to major European cities through Palma de Mallorca Airport (Son Sant Joan Airport). This international airport handles a significant volume of passenger traffic and serves as the primary entry point for visitors. From here, you can easily reach your final destination on the island using various transportation methods.

Buses:

Buses are a popular and cost-effective way to navigate Majorca. The island boasts an extensive bus network operated by the Empresa Municipal de Transports (EMT) and private companies. Key points to know about bus transportation in Majorca:

Palma: The capital city, Palma de Mallorca, has an efficient bus system. Bus routes cover the entire city, including its suburbs and popular tourist areas.

Interurban Buses: For those looking to explore beyond Palma, interurban buses connect the city to various towns and villages across Majorca. These buses are a convenient option for day trips and excursions.

Schedules: Bus schedules can vary, with more frequent services during the tourist season (spring to early autumn). Be sure to check schedules in advance, especially if you plan to travel during off-peak months.

Ticketing: Tickets can typically be purchased on the bus or at designated ticket booths. Some routes also offer discounts for round-trip tickets or multi-day passes.

Trains:

Majorca has a limited but picturesque railway network operated by Serveis Ferroviaris de Mallorca (SFM). Key points to know about train transportation in Majorca:

Historic Trains: The island offers a couple of scenic train rides, such as the famous Sóller Railway that connects Palma to the charming town of Sóller. This journey takes you through stunning mountainous terrain.

Commuter Trains: SFM operates commuter trains connecting Palma with Inca and Sa Pobla, making it convenient for day trips and exploring the interior of the island.

Schedules: Train schedules can be less frequent compared to buses, so plan your trips accordingly.

Taxis:

Taxis are readily available in Majorca and are a convenient way to get around, especially for short distances or when traveling with luggage. Some important details about taxis on the island:

Metered Fares: Taxis in Majorca operate on metered fares. Always ensure that the meter is running to avoid any misunderstandings about the fare.

Availability: Taxis are easy to find in urban areas, at transportation hubs, and tourist spots. However, they may be less abundant in rural areas, so it's wise to plan ahead.

Airport Transfers: Taxis are a popular choice for airport transfers. It's advisable to book a taxi in advance for this purpose, especially during peak tourist seasons.

Car Rentals:
Renting a car in Majorca provides the ultimate flexibility and convenience for exploring the island. Here's what you need to know about car rentals:

Rental Companies: Major international and local car rental companies have offices at

Palma de Mallorca Airport and in major towns. Booking in advance is recommended, especially during the peak season.

Roads and Highways: Majorca has a well-maintained road network, and driving is on the right side. The island's highways are in excellent condition, making it easy to travel between towns and tourist destinations.

Parking: Be mindful of parking regulations in towns and cities. Paid parking is common, and free parking spaces can be limited in popular tourist areas.

Cycling:

Majorca is a popular destination for cyclists due to its scenic routes and pleasant climate. Many visitors choose to rent bicycles to explore the island at their own pace. Bike lanes and routes are well-marked, and there are various bike rental shops across the island.

Ferries and Boat Trips:

If you wish to explore the coastal beauty of Majorca, consider taking a ferry or boat trip. These can take you to neighboring islands, secluded coves, and provide a unique perspective of the island's coastline.

Ferry Services: Regular ferry services operate between Majorca and other Balearic Islands like Ibiza and Menorca. You can also find boat trips for shorter excursions along the coast.

Water Taxis: Water taxis are available in coastal areas and can be a convenient way to reach secluded beaches and small coastal villages.

Walking and Hiking:
For those who love outdoor adventures, Majorca offers numerous hiking and walking trails. These trails range from easy strolls along the coast to challenging hikes in the Tramuntana Mountains. Good hiking shoes and a sense of adventure are all you need to explore these natural wonders.

Transportation within Majorca is diverse and well-suited to the needs of tourists. Whether you prefer the convenience of taxis, the flexibility of renting a car, or the affordability of buses, Majorca offers options for every traveler. Exploring the island's rich landscapes, charming villages, and stunning beaches has never been easier. Plan your transportation accordingly, and you'll be well on your way to enjoying the beauty of this Mediterranean paradise.

• *Safety and Health Tips*

Majorca, the largest of the Balearic Islands in Spain, is a stunning destination known for its beautiful beaches, vibrant nightlife, and rich cultural heritage. Whether you're planning a relaxing beach getaway or an adventure-filled vacation, it's essential to prioritize your safety and health during your trip to Majorca. Here are some vital safety and health tips to keep in mind:

Before You Go:

Travel Insurance: Before embarking on your journey, ensure you have comprehensive travel insurance that covers medical emergencies, trip cancellations, and personal belongings. Check the policy to understand what's included.

Check Travel Advisories: Stay updated with travel advisories from your government or relevant authorities to ensure you're aware of any safety concerns or entry requirements.

Vaccinations and Health Checkup: Consult your healthcare provider to verify if you need any vaccinations or medications for your trip to Majorca. Ensure you're up-to-date on routine vaccinations as well.

During Your Stay:

Stay Hydrated: Majorca enjoys a Mediterranean climate with hot summers. Drink plenty of water to stay hydrated, especially if you're spending time outdoors.

Sun Protection: Protect yourself from the sun's strong rays by wearing sunscreen, sunglasses, and a hat. Sunburn can be severe, and prolonged exposure can lead to heatstroke.

Food and Water Safety: Majorca offers a variety of delicious cuisine, but be cautious when consuming street food or tap water. Stick to bottled water and dine at reputable restaurants to avoid foodborne illnesses.

Language: Learning a few basic Spanish phrases can be helpful in case of emergencies or when seeking assistance.

Emergency Numbers: Familiarize yourself with emergency contact numbers, including the local police, medical services, and your country's embassy or consulate.

Safety Tips:

Stay Aware of Your Surroundings: Be mindful of your belongings and surroundings, especially in crowded tourist areas. Pickpocketing can be a concern in popular destinations.

Secure Your Accommodation: Use hotel safes to store valuable items like passports, jewelry, and extra cash. Lock windows and doors when leaving your room.

Transportation Safety: If you rent a car or use public transportation, adhere to local traffic rules and regulations. Always wear seatbelts and avoid driving under the influence of alcohol.

Beach Safety: When swimming in the beautiful beaches of Majorca, obey posted warning signs and lifeguard instructions. Strong currents can be dangerous.

Nightlife Safety: Majorca is known for its vibrant nightlife, but exercise caution when enjoying the evening. Stay with a group, keep an eye on your drinks, and arrange for a designated driver if necessary.

Healthcare in Majorca:

Medical Facilities: Majorca has well-equipped medical facilities and hospitals, but it's advisable to carry a basic first-aid kit for minor injuries.

Prescriptions: If you require prescription medication, bring an adequate supply along with a copy of your prescription. Pharmacies are widely available, but medications might have different names in Spain.

Emergency Medical Services: In case of a medical emergency, call 112 for assistance. This is the European emergency number that connects you to medical services, fire, or police.

Cultural Sensitivity:

Respect Local Customs: Be mindful of the local culture and customs, especially when visiting religious sites. Dress modestly when required, and avoid loud behavior in quiet areas.

Tipping: Tipping is customary in Majorca, and it's appreciated to leave a small tip for good service in restaurants and cafes.

Noise Levels: Be considerate of noise levels, especially in residential areas, during late hours.

Natural Hazards:

Wildlife and Nature: While Majorca is generally safe in terms of wildlife, it's advisable to be cautious around cliffs, rocky areas, and while hiking. Respect nature and avoid leaving litter behind.

Forest Fires: In the hot summer months, forest fires can be a concern. Follow local advice and fire safety guidelines when visiting natural parks and forests.

Majorca offers a fantastic vacation experience with its stunning landscapes, vibrant culture, and warm hospitality. By following these safety and health tips, you can ensure a smooth and enjoyable trip while prioritizing your well-being. Remember that while exploring this beautiful island, taking precautions and being prepared is key to a memorable and safe adventure in Majorca.

CHAPTER FIVE

Itineraries and Day Trips

• *One-Week Itinerary*

Day 1: Arrival in Palma de Mallorca

Arrive at Palma de Mallorca Airport.
Check-in to your hotel in Palma.
Spend the afternoon exploring Palma's historic Old Town, including the La Seu Cathedral and Almudaina Palace.
Enjoy dinner at a local restaurant in the Old Town.

Day 2: Palma Beaches and Shopping

Head to the beach, such as Playa de Palma or Cala Major.
Relax, swim, or indulge in water sports.
In the afternoon, go shopping on Avenida Jaime III.
Evening at leisure in Palma.

Day 3: Soller and Valldemossa

Take a scenic drive or train ride to Soller.

Explore Soller's charming town center and visit the Port de Soller.

Continue to Valldemossa, known for its picturesque streets and the Valldemossa Charterhouse (Real Cartuja).

Return to Palma for the night.

Day 4: Explore the East Coast

Drive to the eastern coast of Majorca.

Visit the stunning Cala Millor and Cala Ratjada beaches.

Explore the Capdepera Castle and its medieval town.

Return to Palma or stay overnight in the east coast area.

Day 5: Inland Adventure

Explore the Tramuntana Mountains, a UNESCO World Heritage site.

Visit the charming villages of Deià and Fornalutx.

Enjoy hiking or outdoor activities in the area.

Return to Palma for the night.

Day 6: Northern Escapade

Head north to Alcudia and explore its historic old town.
Relax on Alcudia Beach.
Visit the Roman ruins of Pollentia nearby.
Consider a boat trip to Cap Formentor for stunning views.
Return to Palma or stay overnight in Alcudia.

Day 7: Wine Tasting and Departure

Visit a local winery for wine tasting in the Binissalem area.
Explore the vineyards and learn about Majorcan wine production.
Enjoy a farewell lunch.
Depart from Palma de Mallorca Airport.
This one-week itinerary provides a mix of beach relaxation, cultural exploration, and natural beauty, showcasing some of the best that Majorca has to offer. You can adjust it based on your interests and preferences.

•Family-Friendly Activities

Majorca, a gem nestled in the Mediterranean Sea, offers an abundance of family-friendly activities for travelers of all ages. Known for its stunning beaches, rich history, and vibrant culture, Majorca has something to offer every member of the family. In this comprehensive travel guide, we'll explore the top family-friendly activities on this beautiful Spanish island. From beach adventures to historical explorations and thrilling excursions, Majorca promises an unforgettable family vacation.

Beach Bliss

Majorca boasts some of the most beautiful beaches in the Mediterranean. Here, families can bask in the sun, build sandcastles, and take refreshing dips in the crystal-clear waters. Some top family-friendly beaches include:

a. Alcudia Beach: With its shallow waters and soft sand, Alcudia Beach is perfect for families with young children. Water sports and beachfront restaurants add to the allure.

b. Cala Varques: For a more secluded and natural beach experience, venture to Cala Varques. The calm waters are ideal for snorkeling and swimming.

c. Playa de Muro: Known for its Blue Flag status, Playa de Muro offers clean waters and a range of water sports, making it suitable for active families.

Water Parks and Fun
Majorca is home to fantastic water parks that are sure to delight the entire family. Two must-visit options are:

a. Aqualand El Arenal: This water park features a variety of slides, pools, and attractions, ensuring a day filled with aquatic adventures and laughter.

b. Western Water Park: Themed around the Wild West, this park offers thrilling slides, a lazy river, and a wave pool for hours of family fun.

Historical Explorations
Immerse your family in Majorca's rich history and culture through these engaging activities:

a. Bellver Castle: Perched on a hill, this circular castle provides panoramic views of Palma. Explore its history and enjoy the scenic beauty.

b. Palma Cathedral: Known as La Seu, this stunning cathedral is a masterpiece of Gothic architecture. Kids will be awestruck by its grandeur.

c. Historic Train Ride: Hop on the vintage wooden train from Palma to Soller. The journey takes you through picturesque landscapes and charming villages.

Nature Adventures

Majorca's diverse landscapes offer numerous opportunities for nature lovers:

a. S'Albufera Natural Park: A haven for birdwatchers, this wetland park is home to various bird species. Kids can learn about local wildlife while enjoying a peaceful stroll.

b. Caves of Drach: Explore underground caves with impressive stalactites and an underground lake. A classical music concert on the lake is a unique experience for the family.

c. Torrent de Pareis: Hike through the dramatic Torrent de Pareis gorge, surrounded by towering cliffs. It's an adventurous outing for families with older kids.

Adventure and Sports

For families seeking a dose of adrenaline, Majorca offers thrilling activities:

a. Water Sports: From paddleboarding and kayaking to windsurfing and jet skiing, Majorca's coastlines are a playground for water sports enthusiasts.

b. Quad Biking: Explore the island's rugged terrain on quad bikes. There are tours suitable for beginners and experienced riders.

c. Pirate Adventures: Set sail on a pirate ship for an interactive and entertaining family adventure complete with treasure hunts and pirate shows.

Family-Friendly Events
Majorca hosts various family-oriented events and festivals throughout the year. Check the local calendar for celebrations like the Fiesta de Sant Antoni or the Sant Sebastià Festival, which feature parades, music, and traditional food.

Culinary Delights
Introduce your family to the flavors of Majorca with its unique cuisine:

a. Paella: Savor authentic Spanish paella, a rice dish cooked with saffron, vegetables, and your choice of seafood, meat, or both.

b. Ensaimada: Try the sweet and spiral-shaped pastry known as ensaimada, a local delicacy that's sure to please kids and adults alike.

c. Local Markets: Explore local markets like Mercat de l'Olivar in Palma to sample fresh produce, cheeses, and traditional snacks.

Accommodation Options

Majorca offers a wide range of family-friendly accommodations, including beachfront resorts, cozy villas, and charming boutique hotels. Consider your family's preferences and budget when selecting the ideal place to stay.

Majorca is a captivating destination that caters to families seeking adventure, relaxation, and cultural experiences. Whether you're exploring its beautiful beaches, discovering its rich history, or indulging in its culinary delights, Majorca promises an unforgettable family vacation. With a perfect blend of nature, history, and adventure, this Spanish island is an ideal destination for creating lasting memories with your loved ones. So, pack your bags, and get ready to embark on an incredible family adventure in Majorca.

• *Romantic Getaways*

Majorca, also known as Mallorca, is a beautiful Spanish island in the Mediterranean Sea, known for its stunning landscapes, picturesque beaches, and charming villages. It's a perfect destination for couples seeking a romantic escape. Here's a guide to romantic getaways in Majorca:

1. Choose the Right Time to Visit:
Majorca enjoys a Mediterranean climate, making it a year-round destination. However, the best time for a romantic getaway is during the spring (April to June) and fall (September to October) when the weather is pleasant, and the crowds are smaller.

2. Explore Palma de Mallorca:
Start your romantic getaway by exploring the capital city, Palma de Mallorca. Walk hand in hand through the narrow streets of the Old Town (La Lonja) and visit the iconic Palma Cathedral (La Seu). Enjoy a romantic dinner at

one of the many restaurants along the Paseo Marítimo while overlooking the marina.

3. Discover Charming Villages:
Majorca is dotted with charming villages, perfect for romantic day trips. Valldemossa, with its quaint streets and historic buildings, is a must-visit. Sóller, known for its orange groves, offers scenic train rides and beautiful architecture.

4. Relax on Stunning Beaches:
Majorca boasts some of the most beautiful beaches in the Mediterranean. Spend a day lounging on the white sands of Es Trenc Beach, or visit the more secluded Cala Varques for a quiet and romantic day by the sea.

5. Take a Romantic Boat Trip:
Enjoy the Mediterranean together by taking a romantic boat trip. You can book a private sailing tour or join a group excursion to explore hidden coves, snorkel, and enjoy the crystal-clear waters.

6. Wine Tasting in the Vineyards:
Majorca is known for its wine production. Take a tour of the island's vineyards and wineries,

where you can sample local wines and enjoy a romantic picnic amidst the lush vineyards.

7. Hike the Tramuntana Mountains:
For adventurous couples, hiking in the Tramuntana Mountains offers breathtaking views and a chance to connect with nature. The landscapes are particularly stunning during sunrise or sunset.

8. Visit Castles and Historical Sites:
Explore historical sites such as Bellver Castle, a unique circular castle with panoramic views of the city, or the ancient ruins of Pollentia near Alcudia.

9. Enjoy Traditional Cuisine:
Share romantic meals at local restaurants where you can savor traditional Majorcan dishes like paella, sobrassada, and ensaimada. Try a romantic dinner at one of the island's Michelin-starred restaurants for a special culinary experience.

10. Stay in Romantic Accommodations:
Majorca offers a wide range of romantic accommodations, from boutique hotels in the heart of Palma to secluded luxury villas with

private pools. Choose a place that suits your preferences and budget.

11. Sunset Views:
Witnessing a Majorcan sunset with your loved one is a truly magical experience. Head to places like Cap de Formentor or Cala d'Or to watch the sun dip below the horizon.

12. Spa Retreats:
Treat yourselves to a spa day at one of the island's top-notch wellness resorts. Indulge in couples' massages and rejuvenating treatments to enhance your romantic getaway.

13. Attend Local Festivals:
If your visit coincides with a local festival or event, don't miss the opportunity to immerse yourselves in Majorcan culture. Festivals often include traditional music, dance, and food.

Majorca offers the perfect backdrop for a romantic getaway with its stunning natural beauty, rich history, and vibrant culture. Whether you're looking for relaxation on the beach, adventure in the mountains, or simply quality time together, Majorca has something to offer every couple seeking a romantic escape.

•Day Trips to Nearby Islands

Majorca, a stunning gem in the Mediterranean, offers more than just beautiful beaches and vibrant cities. One of the most enticing experiences for travelers is embarking on day trips to nearby islands. These excursions open up a world of natural beauty, culture, and adventure just a short boat ride away. In this Majorca travel guide, we'll take you on a journey to discover the enchanting nearby islands that can be explored in a single day.

1. Dragonera Island: A Natural Paradise

Kickstart your island-hopping adventure with a visit to Dragonera Island, located off the southwest coast of Majorca. The island's name is derived from its unique dragon-like shape. It's a protected natural park, and for good reason. Pristine landscapes, rugged cliffs, and crystal-clear waters make it a haven for nature enthusiasts.

Highlights:

Explore the island's walking trails, leading you through lush pine forests and to panoramic viewpoints.

Don't miss the lighthouse at the western tip, offering breathtaking vistas of the surrounding sea.

Snorkeling and diving opportunities abound in the clear waters teeming with marine life.

2. Cabrera Island: A Marine Reserve Wonderland

Cabrera Island, a short ferry ride from Majorca's southern coast, is a must-visit for those passionate about marine conservation and history. It's a designated national park and marine reserve, making it an ideal destination for ecotourism.

Highlights:

Visit the 14th-century castle that once served as a defense against pirates.

Explore the underwater world with guided snorkeling and diving tours.

Keep an eye out for rare seabirds, dolphins, and the endangered Mediterranean monk seal.

3. Formentera: The Caribbean of the Mediterranean

Known as the "Caribbean of the Mediterranean" for its pristine beaches and azure waters, Formentera is just a short ferry ride from Majorca. This island paradise offers a relaxed atmosphere and is perfect for a day of sun, sea, and sand.

Highlights:

Ses Illetes Beach is a must-visit, known for its powdery white sand and crystal-clear waters.
Explore the charming villages like San Francesc Xavier and Sant Ferran de ses Roques.
Rent a bicycle to explore the island's natural beauty and hidden coves at your own pace.

4. Ibiza: Party Capital Turned Bohemian Hideaway

Ibiza, world-famous for its nightlife, is also an island of natural beauty and culture. Take a ferry from Majorca to explore the island's more tranquil and culturally rich side.

Highlights:

Visit Ibiza Town's historic Dalt Vila, a UNESCO World Heritage site with stunning views.
Explore the hippie markets, such as Las Dalias and Punta Arabí, for unique souvenirs.
Discover secluded beaches like Cala d'en Serra and Cala Salada for a peaceful escape.

5. Menorca: A UNESCO Biosphere Reserve

Menorca, the quieter sibling of Majorca, is a serene getaway for nature lovers. It's renowned for its pristine landscapes and commitment to environmental preservation.

Highlights:

Explore the Camí de Cavalls, a coastal path that circumnavigates the island, offering breathtaking views.
Discover ancient talayots, megalithic stone monuments, and historic towns like Ciutadella.
Enjoy water sports, including kayaking and paddleboarding, in the calm coves.

6. Sa Dragonera Natural Park: A Birdwatcher's Paradise

Sa Dragonera is another hidden gem among the nearby islands of Majorca. This protected natural park is home to diverse bird species and boasts stunning landscapes.

Highlights:

Birdwatchers can spot rare species like Eleonora's falcon and Audouin's gull.
Hike along well-marked trails to discover the island's natural beauty.
Explore the ancient caves and ruins, which provide glimpses into the island's history.

Practical Tips for Island Hopping

Check the ferry schedules and book your tickets in advance, especially during peak tourist seasons.
Pack essentials such as sunscreen, hats, comfortable shoes for walking, and swimsuits.
Respect the natural beauty and wildlife of these islands by following eco-friendly practices and regulations.
Majorca's proximity to these nearby islands offers travelers a diverse range of experiences, from nature exploration to cultural immersion. Plan your day trips wisely, and you'll return to Majorca with unforgettable memories of these

enchanting Mediterranean treasures. Whether you're an adventurer, nature lover, or culture enthusiast, the nearby islands of Majorca have something special to offer every traveler.

CHAPTER SIX

Practical Information

• *Currency and Banking*

The official currency of Majorca is the Euro (€),
just like in the rest of Spain. It's important to
know that Majorca, being a popular tourist
destination, is very accommodating to foreign
travelers when it comes to currency exchange.
You'll find many currency exchange offices
(known as "casa de cambio") at the airport, in
tourist areas, and in most banks.

Banking in Majorca:

Majorca offers a well-developed banking
infrastructure, making it convenient for
travelers to manage their finances. Here are
some key points to note:

Bank Branches: Majorca has numerous banks,
including well-known Spanish banks like
Banco Santander, CaixaBank, and BBVA. You'll
find their branches in major towns and tourist
areas. These banks offer a wide range of
services, including currency exchange, ATM

access, and assistance in English at many locations.

ATMs: ATMs are widely available across the island, including in smaller towns and villages. Most ATMs accept international credit and debit cards, making it easy for travelers to withdraw Euros. However, be aware that some ATMs may charge additional fees for international card usage, so it's a good idea to check with your bank before your trip.

Credit Cards: Majorca is quite credit card-friendly, and major credit cards like Visa and Mastercard are widely accepted in hotels, restaurants, shops, and tourist attractions. However, it's advisable to carry some cash for smaller, local businesses and markets that may not accept cards.

Currency Exchange: While you can exchange currency at banks and exchange offices, be mindful of the exchange rates and any fees involved. It's often more cost-effective to use ATMs for currency withdrawal, as you'll typically receive a competitive exchange rate.

Traveler's Cheques: Traveler's cheques are not as commonly used today as they once were, and you may find it difficult to cash them. It's better to rely on a combination of cash and cards for your financial needs.

Language: Most bank employees in Majorca's tourist areas speak English and are accustomed to assisting international visitors. However, in more remote areas, you may encounter language barriers, so it's helpful to have a basic understanding of common banking terms in Spanish.

Banking Hours: Banks in Majorca generally follow the standard Spanish banking hours, which means they are typically open from 8:30 AM to 2:00 PM on weekdays, with a few branches reopening for a couple of hours in the late afternoon. Some banks may also be open on Saturday mornings, but this can vary by location and time of year.

Majorca provides ample banking and currency exchange options for travelers, making it relatively easy to manage your finances during your visit. It's essential to plan your financial needs in advance and be aware of potential fees associated with currency exchange and ATM withdrawals. Additionally, inform your bank about your travel plans to avoid any issues with card usage abroad.

• *Useful Phrases*

Majorca, the largest of Spain's Balearic Islands, boasts stunning Mediterranean landscapes.
The island's diverse attractions make it a top destination for all types of travelers.
Prepare to be captivated by Majorca's rich culture, cuisine, and natural beauty.

Arrival and Transportation:
4. "¿Dónde está la terminal de llegadas?" - Where is the arrivals terminal?

"Necesito un taxi para ir al hotel." - I need a taxi to go to the hotel.
"¿Dónde puedo alquilar un coche?" - Where can I rent a car?
The island has an efficient bus system for affordable transportation.

Accommodation:
8. "Reservé una habitación doble." - I booked a double room.

"¿Tienen habitaciones disponibles para esta noche?" - Do you have rooms available for tonight?
Majorca offers a range of accommodations, from luxury resorts to charming boutique hotels.

Exploring Majorca:
11. "Me gustaría un mapa de la isla." - I'd like a map of the island.

"¿Cuál es la mejor playa para nadar?" - Which is the best beach for swimming?
"¿Dónde puedo encontrar un buen restaurante local?" - Where can I find a good local restaurant?
The Tramuntana Mountains offer fantastic hiking opportunities.

Cuisine and Dining:
15. "Quisiera probar la paella." - I'd like to try paella.

"Un vaso de vino tinto, por favor." - A glass of red wine, please.
Majorcan cuisine features seafood dishes like "sobrassada" and "ensaimada" pastries.

Local Culture:

18. "¿Cuándo es la fiesta local más cercana?" - When is the nearest local festival?

"¿Dónde puedo ver una actuación de baile flamenco?" - Where can I see a flamenco dance performance?
Embrace the island's traditions, like the Sant Antoni festival and the Castell building tradition.

Safety and Health:
21. "¿Dónde está la farmacia más cercana?" - Where is the nearest pharmacy?

"Necesito asistencia médica." - I need medical assistance.
Majorca is generally safe for tourists, but always be cautious with your belongings.

Beach Tips:
24. "Protector solar es imprescindible en la playa." - Sunscreen is essential at the beach.

"¿Tienen sillas y sombrillas en alquiler?" - Do they have chairs and umbrellas for rent?
Explore the pristine beaches like Playa de Muro and Cala Varques.

Shopping and Souvenirs:

27. "¿Dónde puedo comprar recuerdos locales?" - Where can I buy local souvenirs?

"Me gustaría llevar aceite de oliva de Majorca."
- I'd like to buy Majorcan olive oil.
Look for handicrafts, pearls, and local wines as memorable souvenirs.

Departure:
30. "¿A qué hora es mi vuelo de regreso?" - What time is my return flight?

"¿Dónde está la sala de embarque?" - Where is the departure gate?
Majorca's beauty will stay with you long after you leave.
This guide provides essential phrases and tips to help you make the most of your visit to Majorca. Enjoy your trip to this beautiful Mediterranean island!

• Emergency Contacts

Majorca, the largest of Spain's Balearic Islands, is a breathtaking destination known for its stunning beaches, rich culture, and vibrant nightlife. While visiting this Mediterranean paradise is a dream come true for many travelers, it's essential to be prepared for any unexpected situations. That's where emergency contacts in Majorca come into play. In this comprehensive travel guide, we will explore the vital emergency contacts you should have on hand when visiting Majorca. From medical emergencies to local authorities, we've got you covered.

Medical Emergencies

Emergency Services (112)

In Majorca, as in the rest of Europe, the universal emergency number is 112. Whether you encounter a medical emergency, a fire, or require police assistance, this is the number to dial. The operators are trained to handle various situations and will dispatch the appropriate assistance promptly.

Hospitals

Majorca boasts excellent medical facilities. Some of the top hospitals include:

Son Espases Hospital: Located in Palma, this is a modern hospital with a wide range of medical services.

Hospital de Manacor: Situated in Manacor, this hospital is well-equipped to handle emergencies.
Hospital de Son Llàtzer: Another reliable option in Palma.
Pharmacies

In case of minor health issues or emergencies that don't require a hospital visit, you can turn to local pharmacies. Look for the green cross symbol, and many pharmacies offer 24-hour service on a rotating basis.

Local Authorities

Local Police (092)

For non-emergency issues or if you need to report a crime, you can contact the local police at 092. They are responsible for maintaining public order and safety in Majorca.

Guardia Civil (062)

The Guardia Civil is a law enforcement agency responsible for rural and highway patrol. If you encounter issues outside urban areas, this is the number to call.

Tourist Assistance

Tourist Information (971 19 89 00)

The Tourist Information Office in Majorca provides valuable assistance to visitors. Whether you need guidance on attractions, transportation, or other travel-related inquiries, they are there to help.

Transportation Emergencies

Airport Information (971 78 90 00)

If you experience issues at the Palma de Mallorca Airport or need information about flights, you can contact the airport's information desk directly.

Taxis

In case you lose your belongings or face problems while using a taxi service, keep the contact information of the taxi company you used or the local taxi association handy.

Consulates and Embassies

Consulate or Embassy Contacts

If you're a foreign visitor, it's wise to have your country's consulate or embassy contact information. They can assist with various issues, including lost passports or legal matters.

Local Services

Lost or Stolen Credit Cards

In case your credit cards are lost or stolen, contact your card issuer immediately to report the situation and take necessary action.

Lost or Stolen Mobile Phone

If you lose your mobile phone, contact your service provider to suspend your service and prevent unauthorized use.

Safety Tips for a Secure Stay

Travel Insurance: Before your trip, make sure you have comprehensive travel insurance that covers medical emergencies, trip cancellations, and lost belongings.

Document Copies: Keep photocopies of your important documents, including passports, travel insurance, and driver's licenses, in a separate place from the originals.

Local Currency: Always have some local currency on hand for emergencies or places that may not accept cards.

Communication: Share your itinerary and contact information with a trusted friend or family member back home so they can reach you in case of emergency.

Language: While many people in Majorca speak English and other languages, it's helpful to learn a few basic Spanish phrases to communicate effectively in emergencies.

Exploring the picturesque landscapes and vibrant culture of Majorca is an unforgettable experience. However, being prepared for any unforeseen circumstances is essential to ensure a safe and enjoyable trip. By having these emergency contacts readily available, you can travel with peace of mind, knowing that help is just a phone call away. Remember that prevention is key, so stay informed, take safety precautions, and savor every moment of your Majorcan adventure.

• *Sustainable Travel Tips*

Majorca, the largest of the Balearic Islands in Spain, is a beloved destination for travelers worldwide. Its stunning landscapes, pristine beaches, vibrant culture, and historical sites make it a top choice for vacationers. However, the popularity of this beautiful island has brought about environmental challenges. To ensure the preservation of Majorca's natural beauty and culture for future generations, sustainable travel practices are essential. In this comprehensive travel guide, we will explore sustainable travel tips and eco-friendly activities that will allow you to enjoy Majorca responsibly.

I. Sustainable Accommodation

Choose Eco-Friendly Hotels: Opt for accommodations that have implemented eco-friendly practices, such as energy-efficient lighting, water conservation, and waste reduction.

Boutique and Rural Stays: Consider staying in boutique hotels or rural guesthouses that promote local culture and offer a more authentic experience while supporting local communities.

II. Responsible Transportation

Public Transport: Utilize the island's efficient public transportation system, including buses and trains, to reduce your carbon footprint and traffic congestion.

Rent Electric or Hybrid Vehicles: When renting a car, choose electric or hybrid options to minimize greenhouse gas emissions.

Bike Rentals: Explore Majorca's picturesque landscapes on two wheels by renting bicycles, reducing your environmental impact and staying active.

III. Sustainable Dining

Eat Local: Savor Majorcan cuisine by dining at local restaurants that source their ingredients locally, supporting small-scale farmers and reducing food miles.

Choose Sustainable Seafood: When indulging in seafood, ask for sustainably sourced options to protect the island's marine ecosystems.

IV. Reduce Plastic Waste

Carry Reusable Water Bottles: Bring a reusable water bottle to avoid single-use plastic and help reduce plastic pollution in the island's pristine waters.

Say No to Plastic Bags: Bring your reusable shopping bags when visiting local markets and stores to reduce plastic waste.

V. Respect Natural Environments

Stick to Marked Trails: When hiking or exploring nature reserves, stay on designated trails to protect fragile ecosystems and avoid causing damage.

Leave No Trace: Pack out all waste and dispose of it responsibly to leave nature as beautiful as you found it.

VI. Support Local Culture

Buy Local Souvenirs: Purchase handmade souvenirs and crafts from local artisans to support the island's economy and cultural heritage.

Attend Cultural Events: Experience Majorca's rich cultural traditions by attending local festivals and events, contributing to the preservation of heritage.

VII. Minimize Water Usage

Conserve Water: Be mindful of water usage, especially in arid regions, by taking shorter showers and turning off taps when not in use.

Reuse Towels and Linens: Participate in hotel programs that encourage guests to reuse towels and linens to reduce water and energy consumption.

VIII. Responsible Beach Activities

Clean Up After Yourself: Leave no trash behind on the beaches, and consider participating in local beach clean-up initiatives.

Respect Wildlife: Keep a safe distance from wildlife and refrain from disturbing nesting areas to protect the island's diverse fauna.

IX. Participate in Sustainable Tours

Eco-Friendly Tours: Choose tour operators that prioritize environmental conservation and educate participants on the island's ecosystems.

Explore on Foot: Opt for walking tours to explore Majorca's historic towns and learn about its culture while reducing your carbon footprint.

X. Support Conservation Efforts

Donate to Local Conservation Organizations: Contribute to local environmental groups working to protect Majorca's natural beauty.

Majorca offers travelers an enchanting mix of natural beauty, cultural richness, and recreational activities. To ensure the long-term preservation of this gem in the Mediterranean, it is crucial for visitors to adopt sustainable travel practices. By following the sustainable travel tips outlined in this guide, you can enjoy the beauty of Majorca while minimizing your environmental impact and contributing to the well-being of the island's communities. Remember, responsible tourism is not just about seeing the world; it's about preserving it for future generations to enjoy.

CHAPTER SEVEN

Cultural Insights

•*Majorcan Traditions and Festivals*

Majorca, also known as Mallorca, is the largest of Spain's Balearic Islands and is renowned for its stunning beaches, picturesque landscapes, and vibrant cultural scene. One of the aspects that make Majorca a unique destination is its rich tapestry of traditions and festivals. In this Majorca travel guide, we'll delve deep into the island's cultural heritage and explore the most significant traditions and festivals that define the Majorcan experience.

Majorcan Traditions:

Mallorcan Cuisine: The Majorcan culinary tradition is a true reflection of the island's history and influences. Majorcan cuisine combines Mediterranean flavors with ingredients sourced locally, such as almonds, olives, and seafood. Traditional dishes like "paella," "sobrasada" (a cured sausage), and "tumbet" (a vegetable dish) are a must-try.

Traditional Dress: You can often spot locals wearing traditional Majorcan attire, especially during festivals. Men wear white shirts, black pants, and black shoes, while women don colorful dresses known as "batas" and distinctive headscarves. These outfits are still worn with pride, preserving the island's cultural heritage.

Craftsmanship: Majorca has a strong tradition of craftsmanship, particularly in the production of "roba de llengües" textiles, pottery, and leather goods. Visitors can explore local markets and artisan shops to purchase these handcrafted items as souvenirs.

Gastronomic Festivals: Throughout the year, Majorca hosts numerous food festivals celebrating its culinary traditions. One of the most famous is the "Fira del Fang," a pottery fair in Marratxí, where you can witness potters at work and purchase unique pottery pieces.

Majorcan Festivals:

Sant Sebastià: Celebrated at the end of January, Sant Sebastià is Palma's patron saint festival. It's a vibrant event with parades, live music, and a massive firework display. The atmosphere is electric, making it an excellent time to experience the local spirit.

Semana Santa (Holy Week): Just like in other Spanish regions, Majorca observes Semana Santa with religious processions and events. Palma, in particular, is known for its impressive reenactments of the Passion of Christ.

Fiesta de la Beata: Held in honor of Santa Catalina Tomàs, this festival in Valldemossa is a unique and colorful celebration. Locals dress up in period costumes, and there are music and dance performances throughout the town.

Nit de l'Art: In September, the city of Palma comes alive with art exhibitions, performances, and open galleries during Nit de l'Art. It's a unique way to experience the island's contemporary art scene.

Sant Joan: The summer solstice is celebrated with a bang in Majorca. Bonfires, fireworks, and beach parties take over the island, with the largest celebration happening in the city of Manacor.

Fiesta de la Mare de Déu de la Victoria: On August 15th, the residents of Alcúdia celebrate their patron saint with a grand parade, live music, and traditional dancing. It's a vibrant showcase of Majorcan culture.

Carnival: Majorcan Carnival, celebrated in February, is a time of colorful parades, costumes, and lively street parties. Palma's carnival is the most famous, but you can also find celebrations in other towns across the island.

Revelation of the Three Kings: On January 5th, the arrival of the Three Wise Men is celebrated with parades in towns and cities across Majorca. Children receive gifts from the Kings, and it's a heartwarming family tradition.

Majorca is not just a destination for sun and sea; it's a place deeply rooted in its cultural traditions and festive spirit. The island's blend of historical customs, vibrant festivals, and delicious cuisine make it a unique and captivating destination. Whether you're exploring the quaint streets of Valldemossa during Fiesta de la Beata or dancing in the streets of Palma during Sant Sebastià, Majorca's traditions and festivals offer a glimpse into the heart and soul of this beautiful Mediterranean island. So, immerse yourself in the local culture, savor the flavors, and join the celebrations to create unforgettable memories in Majorca.

•Art and Music Scene

Mallorca, often spelled Majorca, is a stunning island in the Mediterranean Sea, part of Spain's Balearic archipelago. Known for its breathtaking landscapes, beautiful beaches, and vibrant culture, Majorca is also a hub for art and music enthusiasts. In this comprehensive travel guide, we will delve into the island's art and music scene, providing you with insights into galleries, festivals, and local artists that make Majorca a cultural treasure.

Art Scene in Majorca

Majorca's art scene is a fascinating blend of traditional and contemporary influences. Here are some key aspects of the island's art culture:

Pilar and Joan Miró Foundation: Majorca is famous for being the adopted home of the renowned Spanish painter Joan Miró. The Pilar and Joan Miró Foundation, located in Palma de Mallorca, houses a remarkable collection of his artworks. Visitors can explore Miró's studio and gain insights into his creative process while enjoying the island's artistic heritage.

Art Galleries: Palma de Mallorca boasts a thriving art gallery scene. Wander through the charming streets of the Old Town, and you'll find numerous galleries showcasing works by both local and international artists. These spaces provide a platform for contemporary art, making Palma a hotspot for art lovers.

Art Walks: The city also hosts regular art walks, where visitors can explore various galleries and meet the artists behind the creations. It's an excellent opportunity to immerse yourself in the local art scene and perhaps even purchase a unique piece to take home.

Local Artists: Majorca has been home to many talented artists, both past and present. Artists like Santiago Rusiñol and Hermen Anglada Camarasa drew inspiration from the island's landscapes, and their works can still be found in local museums and galleries.

Music Scene in Majorca

Majorca's music scene is diverse and vibrant, catering to a wide range of tastes. Whether you're into classical, electronic, or traditional Spanish music, you'll find something to enjoy on the island:

Classical Music: Majorca has a rich classical music tradition. The Teatre Principal in Palma hosts classical concerts featuring both local and international musicians. Additionally, the annual Chopin Festival in Valldemossa pays tribute to the famous composer who spent time on the island.

Electronic Music: If electronic music is more your style, you're in for a treat. Majorca is known for its vibrant nightlife and electronic music clubs. Venues like Pacha Mallorca and BCM Planet Dance in Magaluf regularly host world-renowned DJs, making the island a hotspot for electronic dance music enthusiasts.

Traditional Spanish Music: Immerse yourself in the local culture by attending traditional Spanish music performances. Flamenco shows are a must-see, and you can find them in various venues across the island. These passionate performances offer a glimpse into Spain's musical heritage.

Music Festivals: Majorca hosts several music festivals throughout the year. The Festival Park of Mallorca in Marratxí is known for its diverse lineup, featuring artists from different genres. Additionally, the Deià International Music Festival, held in the picturesque village of Deià, offers a unique musical experience in a stunning setting.

Where to Experience Majorca's Art and Music Scene

Palma de Mallorca: The capital city is the epicenter of Majorca's cultural scene. Explore the Old Town's narrow streets, home to numerous art galleries, or catch a live music performance at one of the city's many venues.

Valldemossa: This charming village in the Tramuntana Mountains is famous for its association with Frédéric Chopin. Visit the Chopin Museum and attend the annual Chopin Festival for a dose of classical music.

Deià: Known for its artistic community, Deià offers a tranquil setting to enjoy music and art.

The village's stunning landscape has inspired many artists and musicians over the years.

Magaluf: If electronic music is your passion, Magaluf is the place to be. Dance the night away at clubs like BCM Planet Dance and experience the island's energetic nightlife.

Majorca's art and music scene offer a captivating blend of tradition and innovation. Whether you're strolling through art galleries in Palma, attending a classical concert in Valldemossa, or dancing to electronic beats in Magaluf, the island has something to offer every art and music enthusiast. Majorca's rich cultural heritage and breathtaking landscapes make it an ideal destination for those seeking a harmonious blend of artistic experiences and natural beauty.

•*Majorcan History and Heritage*

Majorca, also known as Mallorca, is the largest of the Balearic Islands in the Mediterranean Sea and boasts a rich history and heritage that spans millennia. This Majorca travel guide will take you on a journey through the island's captivating past, vibrant culture, and stunning natural landscapes, offering insights into its historical significance and the attractions that make it a top destination for travelers.

I. Ancient Roots and Phoenician Influence

Majorca's history dates back to the prehistoric era, with evidence of human settlements dating as far back as 3000 BC. The island's strategic location in the Mediterranean made it a prized possession for various civilizations, including the Phoenicians, who established trading posts here around 600 BC. They were followed by the Carthaginians and then the Romans.

II. Roman Legacy and the Foundation of Palma

During Roman rule, Majorca prospered, and the city of Palma, known as "Palmaria Palmensis" at the time, was founded. The Romans built roads, bridges, and aqueducts, leaving an enduring architectural legacy that can still be seen in Palma today. The island thrived as an agricultural center, producing olive oil, wine, and grain for the Roman Empire.

III. Byzantine and Moorish Influences

After the fall of the Roman Empire, Majorca was briefly ruled by the Byzantines before falling under the control of the Moors in the 8th century. The Moors left a profound mark on the island, introducing irrigation systems and crops like oranges, almonds, and rice, which continue to be major agricultural products in Majorca.

IV. Reconquista and Christian Rule

In the 13th century, Majorca became a focal point of the Christian Reconquista. King James I of Aragon successfully recaptured the island in 1229, ending nearly 300 years of Moorish rule. This marked the beginning of Majorca's Christian era, and the island's culture began to evolve under Catalan influence.

V. The Age of Exploration

During the Age of Exploration, Majorca played a significant role as a maritime and trading hub. The island's capital, Palma, became a thriving port city, attracting merchants, explorers, and artists. Gothic and Renaissance architecture flourished during this period, and numerous palaces and churches were built.

VI. Pirate Raids and Fortifications

Majorca's strategic location made it susceptible to pirate attacks in the 16th and 17th centuries. The island's coastline is dotted with fortresses and watchtowers built to defend against these threats. Today, many of these fortifications have been preserved and offer visitors a glimpse into Majorca's turbulent past.

VII. Modern Era and Contemporary Culture

Majorca continued to evolve through the modern era, experiencing periods of prosperity and hardship. In the 20th century, it became a popular tourist destination, attracting visitors from around the world. Today, tourism is a vital part of the island's economy, and Majorca is known for its vibrant culture, stunning beaches, and welcoming atmosphere.

VIII. Majorcan Cuisine and Gastronomy

Majorcan cuisine is a reflection of the island's history and geography. Traditional dishes include paella, sobrassada (a spicy sausage), and ensaimada (a sweet pastry). Majorca's Mediterranean climate also makes it an ideal place for vineyards, producing quality wines like Malvasia and Manto Negro.

IX. Festivals and Traditions

Majorca's cultural heritage is celebrated through a variety of festivals and traditions. The Fiestas de San Juan in June involves bonfires and fireworks to mark the summer solstice, while the Festa des Vermar in September celebrates the grape harvest with parades and wine tastings. Traditional folk dances and music are an integral part of these festivities.

X. Major Attractions and Activities

Now that we've delved into Majorca's history and heritage, let's explore some of the top attractions and activities you can enjoy on this beautiful island:

Palma Cathedral (La Seu): This iconic Gothic cathedral is a must-visit, showcasing stunning architecture and history.

Bellver Castle: A 14th-century circular castle offering panoramic views of Palma and the surrounding area.

Serra de Tramuntana: This UNESCO World Heritage-listed mountain range is perfect for hiking and exploring picturesque villages like Valldemossa and Deià.

Coves del Drach: Explore these mesmerizing limestone caves with an underground lake and stalactites.

Beaches: Majorca boasts numerous beautiful beaches, including Playa de Palma, Cala Millor, and Cala Varques, perfect for swimming and water sports.

Sóller and the Vintage Train: Take a scenic vintage train ride from Palma to Sóller, a charming town known for its orange groves.

Local Markets: Visit local markets like Mercat de Santa Catalina and Mercat de l'Olivar to sample fresh produce and artisanal goods.

Wine Tasting: Discover Majorca's wine culture by visiting wineries in the Binissalem-Mallorca region.

Water Parks: If you're traveling with family, you can enjoy water parks like Aqualand El Arenal and Western Water Park.

Mallorcan Nightlife: Experience the vibrant nightlife in Palma, with bars, clubs, and live music venues.

Majorca's history and heritage are as diverse and captivating as its landscapes. From ancient civilizations to modern tourism, the island has seen it all, leaving a cultural tapestry that continues to enchant visitors. Whether you're drawn to its historical sites, natural beauty, or culinary delights, Majorca offers a unique and memorable travel experience that combines the best of the past and present. So pack your bags, embark on your Majorca adventure, and let the island's rich history and heritage inspire your journey.

CHAPTER EIGHT

•*Conclusion*

In conclusion, Majorca is a captivating destination that offers a perfect blend of natural beauty, vibrant culture, and a myriad of activities for travelers of all tastes. Whether you're seeking relaxation on pristine beaches, exploring historic towns, indulging in delicious cuisine, or embarking on outdoor adventures, Majorca has it all. With its warm Mediterranean climate, friendly locals, and diverse landscapes, this island in Spain promises unforgettable experiences for every visitor. So, pack your bags and get ready to discover the enchanting allure of Majorca – a place where relaxation and adventure harmoniously coexist in a paradise waiting to be explored.

Printed in Great Britain
by Amazon

36606433R00099